How to
Analyze
People

Daniel Mind

How to Analyze People
Read Body and Mind

ISBN: **9781089128335**

TABLE OF CONTENTS

INTRODUCTION

To daily decipher our destructive thoughts may seem like a task with no end in sight, due to the huge amount of data that goes through our brains on a daily basis. Especially when we grow up to believe that what we perceive is the way the world is. It is very easy to react as a simple programmed computer towards any situation we meet in life, but to replace this reaction with a respond of awareness demands a whole heap of effort. At least in the beginning when we try to carry out this new method of alertness into our subconscious mind, but with practice we can make perfection.

We live in a world where the mass of people stand before choices and decisions they want, or need to make. Our thoughts influence our emotions and these influence the actions we take, as well as the decisions involved in making them. Paradoxically, we often do not analyze our thoughts before we let them go ahead into our subconscious thinking. This therefore could allow negative thoughts to slip into our subconscious mind, which as a result creates a negative feeling in our body system. Without realizing this we then continue on with our daily lives, while our body system is in disharmony and not aligned with the path we think we are progressing on.

Being in this state, we could easily view our outer world as the cause of our uncomfortable feeling. At the same time the effort and energy used in trying to change this while being in this mental state, shall often not deliver us the required results. As an extreme example; it could go so far that when destructive thoughts cross our minds, we might think of these as our natural habitual thoughts and create a culminating believe that destruction is our human nature. Yet, nothing could be further away from the truth than this very thought itself! An extremely negative thought pattern which we all should consider avoiding at all times, for the sake of our own benefit.

In fact and perhaps also unfortunately, the more people on our earth who actually imply this negative thought as truth or reality, the worse it will become for the future of our earth and everything on it. That is because life reflects to us the reality, we imagine it to be. So if we truly believe that life is nothing more than an eternal damnation, we should expect nothing else from it than just that!

Therefore studying how we can change this condition is far better than continuing to blindly react to situations. Let us just take a moment, to think about this concept as best as we can; because in this endeavor lies the opportunity for us to regain control to the operating technique of our subconscious mind, which when controlled appropriately is the greatest power within ourselves. This will enable us to control our actions and make the differences, we wish to bring forth.

Changing our outer world, if we are not satisfied with it is not going to be achievable.

This is why we have to focus our attention on changing our inner world. And in doing so, at the same time we positively influence our outer world in creating the opportunities we wish to have.

The common goal of all humankind is to live in a better world. A better world also means, a world where more and more of our world's population start enjoying the greatest □ualities of life.

Practicing the habit of directing our subconscious mind will eventually raise the awareness and importance of thought observation. Our life becomes much more interesting on a personal level, when we realise how we can influence our own reality. A peaceful and calm mind ultimately gives us a healthy physical body. Where stress is reduced or replaced with excitement, and a healthy enthusiasm for exploring more life through inner happiness.

What has happened is now in the past, and little to noting can be done to change our past. However the present and the future are totally in our control. Hence, if we wish to receive the greatest reward in life, it is time we start concentrating about what we spend our days thinking about. We can train ourselves to ac□uire new habits regardless of the circumstances that surround us, because our positive thoughts can stimulate us to take positive actions to create positive circumstances for us. That can deliver us success of such great magnitude, which we never might have thought was personally achievable.

CHAPTER 1

THE HUMAN MIND

The human mind is the most incredible computer it would be possible to imagine. Yet no one knows where it is! Scientists have made detailed studies of the brain, but have been unable to locate where the mind is.

Our brain is composed of some 14 trillion brain cells! A very few people are making use of perhaps less than 10% of their mental capability. Most of us are probably using nearer 1%. So the potential we have is virtually unlimited.

For our purposes, imagine that the brain is in two parts: the Conscious mind and the Subconscious (or Inner) mind. The conscious mind does all our day to day thinking, our communication with others and general thoughts each day of our lives. Do you realise that you are thinking at the rate of about 1,200 words a minute?

The Subconscious mind looks after all our involuntary functions: the beating of our hearts, the breathing of our lungs. It also has stored in it every single experience and every thought we have ever made from the moment we were born. Some people believe that it also contains all the memories of our past lives as well. As it contains memories of everything that has ever happened, we can use it to locate information we need. For instance, you may be walking down the street and suddenly bump into someone you haven't seen for a long while. Whilst talking, you are frantically thinking of their name, and suddenly it will come to you, hopefully whilst your are still in conversation!

If it is something that occurred many years ago, your subconscious mind may have to spend a long time locating the necessary information. That is why we can sometimes have a problem when we go to bed. In the morning the answer will suddenly pop into our heads.

Admittedly, it doesn't work exactly the way we want it to. Yet our brain is perfect, it remembers and files away everything. Sometimes, though, our recall is faulty. When something is "on the tip of our tongue" our brain is not working as well as we would like it ot. The best way to handle this is to temporarily "forget" what we are trying to remember and soon it will come back to us whilst we are thinking about something completely different. If you are constant absent-minded, it would pay to take a memory training course. (contact me)

There is a third part of our mind also. This is the Super-Conscious mind. Hardly anything is known about it, but this is where everything really important happens. Ideas come from here. So does creativity, and ESP. (Extra Sensory Perception) When you come up with a good idea, it comes directly from your Super-Conscious mind, through your Sub-Conscious mind to your Conscious mind, and it is then up to you to act upon it.

Your Super-Conscious mind is your creative force, and is the most important part of your mind. It contains all the answers to anything you may ever want to know. Writers, artists, composers, inventors, clairvoyants, and all sort of other people use this part of their mind when doing whatever it is they do. Sometimes these people feel totally inspired.

A composer may start on a melody and then, all of a sudden, the rest of the tune just comes with no apparent effort on his part. It has all come from directly from the Super-Conscious mind.

Your Super-Conscious mind contains all the information of the universe and you have access to it whenever you want. All you have to do is ask.

You have already used it many, many times. Say, for instance, that you have a major problem that has to be resolved the following day. You worry about it and think about it, and find it hard to get to sleep as it is still bothering you. When you wake up the following morning, the answer suddenly pops into your head. "Eureka" you cry and you happily go and solve the problem. Where did the answer come from? You did not have it when you fell asleep. It was not in your Conscious mind, nor was it in your Sub-Conscious.

What happened was, while you were asleep, the Sub-conscious contacted the Super-Conscious mind and asked for the answer. Next time you have a problem of this sort, tell your Sub-Conscious mind about it and say that you need an answer by a certain time.

Overnight is fine, but two days would be better. Don't tell it how you want the problem resolved. Just ask for the answer and confidently expect it to come. Ask again several times during the time limit you have set, and your Super-Conscious mind will solve your problem.

UNCOVERING THE SECRETS ON HOW TO READ MINDS

The Brain and the Mind

The brain is the central command post of every human activity; each and every bodily activity finds directives from the brain. The physical brain is divided into two hemispheres namely the right and the left hemispheres; each hemisphere has uni□ue functions for the total body performance. The hemisphere further divide into smaller organs such as the hypothalamus and the frontal cortex lobe, all which have distinctive functions for message relays and effective brain neuron chemical production which are effective for better functioning of the brain. The mind on the other hand is the intangible part of the brain, the mind reasons, thinks and acts in relation to the physical functioning of the brain. The mind states are defined in two terms which are the conscious mind and the subconscious mind. The conscious mind is the aware part of the mind thoughts processed in this state of the mind happens in full awareness of the individual concerned. Research has it that this part of the brain processes 10 percent of any given event. The subconscious mind on the other hand represented the unaware state of mind by definition this part of the mind is concealed from the conscious state. Paradoxically speaking this state of the mind processes more 90 percent of any event, this state of the mind is more awake when the conscious is at rest. People who engage in how to read minds studies affect this part of the brain more.

Are mind reading theories true?

An individual can read minds, however the act in itself needs lots of concentration and soul bonding, for instance a person reading minds certainly affects high concentration subconsciously to link bonding with the contact individual. Most people who can affect this level of concentration can communicate efficiently through telepathy. Attaining this level needs guidance and unbiased information and facts about how one can actually achieve the act. Training the mind to achieve telepathy is possible through certain laws of attraction fits.

Laws of attraction and mind reading

Law of attraction can be simple yet effective in helping individuals attain different self development acts. Laws of attraction means of attaining self development acts involve certain acts such as positive thinking. Your ability in telling yourself you can do impossibilities doubles up to be the opening door for whatever act you wish to affect. Most people known to do accurate mind readings have different ways of interpreting an individual's mind.

Some of this people will focus their mind to yours and through telepathy and other universal laws they can be able to tell in accuracy whatever you thinking about, others will ask question randomly and from that tell you things about your life. Some people tend to liken this to psychics powers, they maybe right in some degree but the kind of mind reading that comes from law if attraction is purely intuitive. How to read mind lessons can be attained through concentration and learning to listening to yourself first before you engage any external mind readings.

HOW TO READ A MIND

Do some people really know how to read a

mind?

Let me start by saying that each of us has that 'personal private space' which we call our thoughts. Our physical privacy can be violated. Someone may look through the keyhole of your bedroom as you change your clothes. Someone may scan the messages in your inbox without you knowing it. Someone can even go as far as snoop in your bedroom, looking for your oh-so-treasured diary where you express your most utmost feelings. All these are manifestations of your physical privacy being violated. It does happen, and it doesn't show signs of not happening in the near future.

But how about our minds? Can people (not literally) open our minds and read what it contains? Can you look at someone's eyes for 20 seconds, stare deep enough in those pupils and actually reach his mind? Is it really possible? Where science can bombard you with scientific terminologies and theories that are sure to confuse you, here are ordinary answers which hopefully, can shed some light into this issue. At the end is a realization that you have hopefully found after reading this book.

First thing's first: The person whose mind you attempt to read must not want his mind to be read. It's useless to read his mind if he is more than willing to freely express his thoughts. In this case, you wouldn't be needing tips on how to read a mind. Once you've established that the person really does not want you to read his mind, proceed by asking the simple ☐uestions.

For instance, if you're married, and it's already 2 in the morning and your partner hasn't come home yet, once he or she actually arrives home, DO NOT bombard him with intrusive ☐uestions. Instead, ask him simple, plain ones. You can begin by asking "So, how was the event you attended?"

By asking questions like these, your partner wouldn't get the impression that you're trying to investigate his coming home late. He would feel that you're actually just plainly asking. Couple this ⬜uestion with a smile, and it's more than probable that your partner would feel that you're really just asking, not probing.

If asking simple ⬜uestions does not cut it, you can switch to using simple caring statements. Sweet nothings like "I was beginning to be worried. You should have texted me" can really do the trick and s⬜ueeze the truth out of someone. These heart-wrenching lines, whether you really meant them or not, are almost guaranteed to make a person spill his beans.

One thing has to be made clear here: The two methods expressed here are not fool-proof ways on how to read a mind. In reality, there hasn't been a proven way to read a person's mind. There is a reason why each person's 'personal private space' remains exactly that - 'personal and private' - after thousands of years of human existence. These methods are just less intrusive (thus more effective) ways of forcing the truth out of someone who's determined to hide it. After all, sometimes knowing the truth beats the hell out of having some mystical mind reading power.

TIPS FOR USING MEDITATION TO MASTER THE HUMAN MIND

For centuries, people from different cultures have used meditation to master the human mind. From its esoteric roots among Eastern mystics to its contemporary status among diverse cultures, the practice is now accepted by mainstream society. Still considered a spiritual practice, it is also recognized by secular sources as both as a mode of relaxation and a means of achieving goals.

In order to understand how meditation works, it is necessary to know how the conscious and the subconscious minds work. The conscious mind is the thinking part of the brain that sets goals and determines the steps needed to reach them. Although it is great with ideas, it gets distracted and jumps from one thought to another every few seconds. At any one time, it can only store a few pieces of information and is unable to retain most of them.

The subconscious mind, on the other hand, can remember unlimited bits of information for an entire lifetime and is connected to the conscious mind through the five senses. This is the part of the brain that responds to subliminal suggestions and sees the big picture. It can actually accomplish the goals of the conscious mind, but it must first receive the messages from the conscious brain in order to act on them. Meditation helps to develop the strong neural pathways that allow this to happen.

Since the subconscious is unable to distinguish reality from the imagination, it thinks whatever it visualizes is real. The brain, in other words, is wired to act on the beliefs of the subconscious - whether they are positive or negative. The good news is that the subconscious can be programmed to manifest success by changing the way the mind works, and meditation is the tool that allows it to happen.

The brain vibrates at different frequencies, based on its actions at any given moment. There are five kinds of brain waves:

• Beta - the thinking brain, alert and tense

• Alpha - physical and mentally relaxed, but aware

• Theta - conducive to meditation, memory, intuition; reduced consciousness

• Delta - dreamless sleep, deep meditation, healing; unconsciousness

• Gamma - increased compassion; optimal cognitive function; conscious awareness of reality

The act of meditation not only creates an atmosphere for the brain to work more effectively; when compared in studies to similar activities - such as relaxation or resting - meditation also produces more changes in brain waves. Science has finally proven what monks knew thousands of years ago. Meditation is the key to mastering the mind.

HOW TO READ PEOPLE'S MINDS - 3 SECRET WAYS TO READ PEOPLE'S THOUGHTS

While we haven't yet reached the age of flying cars and robot wars, we have at least reached the point where we know how to read people's minds. These days, there are various methods you can use to know what another person is thinking.

These methods range from the basic to the scientific. If you want to explore the knowledge of how to read people's minds, check out some of these tips below.

Body Language

One of the basic ways on how to read people's minds is by reading their body language. As primitive as this method might seem, not a lot of people seem to know about it or know how to actually use it. However, I'll let you in on some of the key bodily movements that can help you read people's minds.

When talking to a person, notice the direction that their knees are pointed. If the knees are turned towards you, then you know that the other person is interested in you and agrees with what you're saying. On the other hand, it they're turned away from you, then you better think of a way to capture their interest we will discause more about this in the chapter below.

Eye Movement

Here's how to read people's minds through their eyes. When a person is trying to create an image out of nothing, they will most likely look upward and to the left.

In the meantime, a person trying to remember a particular image will most likely look upward and to the right. As effective as this method is, don't let it be the last straw when making a decision.

Brain Activity

On a more scientific scale, there has been a small yet significant progress when it comes to knowing how to read people's minds. Neuroscientist Kendrick Kay, along with his colleagues, has stumbled upon a way to determine which image a person is looking at without ever seeing the images before.

According to "Scientific American," the team was able to create a computer model that could read a person's brain activity accurately. That model could read the brightness and angle the person perceived when looking at the picture; so when the series of pictures was presented to the model, it was able to determine which picture the person was looking at by comparing its brightness and angle. Of course, the model is not 100% right all the time as some pictures may have similar amounts of brightness and angle.

Learning how to read people's minds can be interpreted in many, different ways. While we haven't yet reached the point where reading people's minds is as easy as looking above their heads and reading words from a thought bubble, we have at least made it halfway there.

WHAT DOES IT TAKE TO BECOME A MIND READER?

Can a mind reader accurately read the mind of another person? The answer to this □uestion depends on how you understand and interpret this □uestion. It was once said that no one can read the mind of a man even the devil knoweth not the thoughts of a man. Devil in this statement means your spiritual leader and man denotes the female as well as the female gender. What goes on or is going on in the mind of a person is always difficult to ascertain accurately.

Even the mind reader experts and researchers only attempt to the read the mind of a person through the actions, emotions, expressions, behavior and even facial expressions of that person. In essence it is not reading the mind but relying on other factors to predict what a person may be thinking about. The following are some of the methods in which mind readers apply to ascertain what a person may be thinking about; note the words here, 'may be thinking' but not 'thinking' about. All minding reading techniques are faced by challenges and limitations and re□uire super mind power to read the mind of a person accurately.

By looking at the movement of lips when one is deeply thinking about something, you can ascertain what one is thinking about. The only difficulty here is that you are required to observe the movement of the lips when the person is not aware that you are doing so and this is easy. Movement of lips is a reflex action and most people are not aware that they move their lips when deeply thinking about something and this can show their emotions, thoughts and feelings at the moment. Most people move their lips when talking and this may not however indicate thinking, it sig god that you consider the surrounding circumstances when you want to ascertain the thinking of a person from its movement of lips.

The color and movement of the eyes coupled with facial expression may also give you a clue on what one is feeling or thinking at that moment. Red eyes are an indicator of anger and frustration while bight wide open eyes may signify anxiety or fear depending on the circumstances. There is a theory (or is it a myth?) that the pupils in the eyes of a human being when someone sees something which he or she likes or is in high desire of something. Proponents of this theory believe that one a person of an opposite sex approaches another and his or pupils get larger, that is a show of love.

It is very simple to become a mind reader by listening to people's thoughts, opinions and believes because people talk mostly on what is in their minds. Secondly, look at the movement of the eyes; people who are interested in what you are saying usually give you a direct close eye contact. Those disinterested in you or whatever you are talking about may look away or look sleepy. Movement of the eyes is mostly coupled with facial expressions and it is a good indicator of the thoughts of a person as stated above

CHAPTER 2

POSITIVE THINKING - THE POWER OF THE HUMAN MIND

The power of the human mind has been regarded as one of the most powerful in our universe. Just like what most people say, it's always mind over matter. Just think and it will happen - think positive and everything will be alright. It's the same as waking up at the wrong side of the bed, and the whole day follows along with it - you being irritated, angry, tired and every negative feeling or situation. But by waking up at the right side of the bed, you end up being productive in work, feeling good about yourself...and everything else. Being optimistic may prove to be very beneficial in our day-to-day lives. It's thinking that it will be like this and it will be - the Law of Attraction. But this power can also be destructive for us. But exactly how can this be possible? It's the moment when you become pessimistic.

The Law of Attraction has had many followers and critics over the past years. But what is it? It's simply saying that you should know what you want, think about it, ask for it, and eventually you will get it. Its roots say that it was from Quantum Physics, and has been popularized by a film in 2006 "The Secret" which was then made into a book. When you think about it for a second, it's actually making the power of the human mind work its wonders. The Law of Attraction is the power that we all have in our minds - something that we have been using for our whole lives. Have you ever stopped and thought that, "Yeah, it's a lucky day for me," and all the things that had happened to you that day were indeed a stroke of luck?

Maybe it is, but it's actually you who put yourself into it. You thought of it - you activated the whole universe to support you into making it a reality. It's the same when you were wearing that new pair of white pants and some guy splashed coffee on you - and the list goes on that seemingly unlucky day. Why did it happen? Because you started to think that, "oh damn, I guess it isn't my day today."

A number of people have adapted this Law of Attraction by putting it into different schools of thoughts & books and areas of studies, such as Napeleon Hill's "Think and Grow Rich" and even in Theosophy, but all of them come to one point: positive thinking. Though it also received a number of criti☐ues across the world saying that if you just need to know what you want, visualize it et al, then why are there still poverty and suffering in the world? Maybe because, for example, those people who are stuck in poverty had always thought that they will be poor forever - they do not exert any effort. They do not even think that it will be good in the future - they use the power of the human mind in a different way - in an awful way into thinking that there is nothing for them in the future. But you have your choice as you read this - and it would be a great way to now stop, think and visualize of the positive things, for your good and the goodness of the whole society.

CAN THE HUMAN MIND IN SEARCH FOR UNDERSTANDING FIND THE ANSWERS IT SEEKS IN PATTERNS?

It has been said that "everyone is searching for something," and in further scrutiny of that famous quote, well, that sounds about right doesn't it? Searching for what you ask? Who knows, each person and mind is unique, although there are of course common things that folks search for; soul mates, the meaning of life, and lately, I guess we still have a huge number searching for employment. Okay so, I'd like to discuss the philosophical notion that the human brain uses patterns and similarities to make sense of the world around them.

Now then, can the Human Mind in its

omnipresent search for understanding, find the answers it seeks in the re-occurring patterns it senses? Well, consider how the brain works and how it learns. We all see things, experience, and observe and we commit much of this to memory, through trial and error we learn to deal with our environment, learn a new skill, or solve a problem we are presented with, thus, pattern recognition is extremely important in all we do. Hopefully we learn from our mistakes, especially the ones that knock us into the dirt or cause a serious or dangerous challenge.

Another interesting thing we know is that those with extremely high IQs often see patterns or anomalies that others inherently miss. Does that mean high IQ individuals learn faster too, that is to say will learn faster from their mistakes, or recognize less-than-positive signs first? If patterns are a clue to the answers we seek, wouldn't it also stand to reason that the human mind with the best ability to see patterns will also be able to make sense of the world, their environment, and surroundings faster, perhaps come up with novel solutions, or cross-pollinate in their minds to come across a new discovery, one which others mistakenly over looked?

The answers to all those questions should be in the affirmative, if my logic here holds to reason, for which I haven't found any flaws as I progress in this dialogue with you here today. My suggestion for those who want to find answers is to study the patterns and anomalies, and in those observations you will find the answers you seek to make sense of the world around you and answer all your □uestions. Well, at least that's one of the ways I do it, and it seems to work for me.

Indeed, if you'd like to consider this in greater depth, I am open for a philosophical dialogue on this topic, so maybe we should talk?

THE SECRET POWER OF THE HUMAN MIND

As soon as you start caring about the meaning of your dreams you open a door that leads you to a new level of consciousness, where you start noticing various aspects of your daily reality that you didn't care about before.

You learn how to understand the development of reality, and therefore you are able to make predictions. Many times you cannot see too much, while there is always the wise unconscious mind's plan, behind your own plans, guiding you in the darkness of your ignorance through dream messages, even when you cannot see the end of the road yet.

If you precisely follow the unconscious' guidance in dreams, you acquire a secret power derived from your own mind, even though it doesn't belong to you: the wise unconscious mind that produces your dreams is not part of your brain. It regulates the functionalism of your body and sends you protective messages in dreams, helping you transform the wild and dangerous side of your conscience into human, and at the same time, completely develop your intelligence.

You receive secret lessons and you have a communication with the unconscious mind that answers your ⬚uestions in dreams, once you learn the dream language.

There are millions of dream interpreters in our world, but only the psychiatrist Carl Jung was able to discover the exact way to translate the mysterious dream language, after long research and many experiments, comparisons and therapies.

I could prove that he was correct by precisely following his method and discovering much more. I completed his research, giving to the world all the answers that he could not give, because he stopped in the middle of the journey. He was afraid to continue, since he knew that there is craziness a priori inside the human brain.

This absurd content is inherited: it is not the result of personal experiences, as Jung discovered after analyzing the words and phrases used by patients that suffered from grave mental illnesses.

The mission of the unconscious mind that produces your dreams is exactly to protect you from your wild side and help you overcome the absurdity you are born with.

However, since you have precious information about all the crucial points of your life, this protection gives you a secret power. Only by translating the meaning of your own dreams, you have objective information about other people and especially about yourself, and your life, being able to prepare the future results you desire.

I simplified Jung's method of dream interpretation, transforming it into a practical method of dream translation that everyone easily learns, and starts immediately seeing positive results with all the notions they have.

You'll invest a small amount and a short period of time in order to study the dream language, and then have access to the wisdom and the guidance of the unconscious mind in your dreams for the rest of your life.

This is an investment to your advantage without a doubt, since you'll see dreams forever, the same way you do now, and the secret power that this knowledge gives you is a tool that opens many other doors for you in your daily life.

HOW TO READ PEOPLE'S MINDS - THE SECRET TRICKS TO READ PEOPLE'S THOUGHTS

One of the greatest mysteries of mankind is discovering the secret to how to read people's minds. If you could read people's thoughts you could know exactly what another person is thinking. The power of mind reading tricks and techniques really lies in your ability in how you are reading the behavior and signals that the other person gives you. Here are the secret ways to read people's thoughts through body language. When you know what a person is thinking, you are in possession of powerful knowledge that can help you lead interaction in your favor.

Reading body language is easy and fun. Most of us don't do this consciously, so we fail to recognize just what a great mind reading technique it is. Here are some things to watch out for to get you started:

* If they are facing you, they are listening and paying attention to you. But if they are turned away, they are not focused on you. If they are rocking side to side, they are impatient and want to end the conversation.A turned back is a sign of deliberately ignoring or avoiding someone.

* When someone backs up, on a subconscious

level they feel threatened and are retreating from you.If someone is gradually moving towards you, they are interested in you or what you are saying.

* Pointing their knees or their feet towards you is a universal sign they are in agreement with you, they are aligning their posture to yours.

* If they begin to mimic your body language, that is a sign that you are leading the conversation.

* -Crossed arms are a sign of defensiveness or contempt, the exception is when the thumbs are clearly visible and pointing upwards, that means they are feeling detached but amicable.

* If their hands are facing you with open palms, then they are open/receptive to what you are saying.

* If eyes look upward to the left they are trying to create an image out of nothing. They are actively using their imagination, this can be a sign that they are making up whatever they are telling you.If their eyes look upwards to the right, they are trying to remember a particular image, access a specific memory. These are just the usual guidelines, some people, especially the left-handed, have the opposite eye movements so it's important to get a baseline reading by compelling them to remember something that you know happened

Most of these things we will feel during our interactions. Without paying conscious attention, we will start to feel when a person is becoming defensive and only then notice their closed body language. Learning to pay attention to your feelings is an easy way to start becoming more aware of what the body language of others is telling you.

Aside from sociopaths and habitual liars, deception is stressful. When we are stressed out blood circulation is prioritized to the essential organs and diverted away from the extremities. If someone is lying, they are very likely to have cold hands. This stress will also make the person more jumpy in response to a loud noise or some other startle. But just remember, stress does not imply deception.

Eye contact when we are lying is not natural, but it can be forced. If a person starts making strange eye contact that feels off, then they are probably angling something shady.

The way a person is thinking will be reflected in the words they use and the □uestions they ask. Someone who is likes to talk about social situations and relationships is someone who is very focused on interpersonal relationships and will respond much better to interactions that incorporate those elements. Relationships are based on emotions and these people will be swayed more by emotional arguments than logical ones.

By paying attention to all the signs a person is

unknowingly giving off, you will seem to be reading their mind. These techniques will give you an awareness of what others are thinking that you may even start to surprise yourself with your accuracy. Most people are so focused on what they are about to say next or what they want out of an interaction that they are only diverting a very small amount of their attention to the other person. When we focus our full attention on what the other person is doing and saying, we gain tremendous insight into not only what they are thinking, but how they think.

HOW BARRIERS HELP THE HUMAN MIND AND THOUGHTS

The Human mind is always at work. It is through our thoughts that we function from day to day. The decisions that we make as well as our behaviour can be right or wrong, proper or improper as we are not perfect.

Some of these behaviours can be categorized as follows:

Those that are important to remain right with God and are essential for the Christian to remain on the right path i.e. love for God and obedience. These ought to be done on the person's own free will.

Worthwhile actions that keep the Christian focused and strengthens his faith, like regular bible study, church attendance and doing good for others.

Then there are those thoughts and behaviours that are not befitting of a believer, but are not sinful. For e.g. drinking of alcohol, sexual fantasy or hanging out in clubs. Even though these are not necessarily sinful in nature, if gotten out of control can lead the believer into sin.

Sinful and Unethical Actions. These thoughts and actions should not be entertained at all by the Christian.

The Barriers

There are barriers to prevent the Christian believer from stepping out and being placed in a situation where his mind can be controlled and therefore be manipulated. From the very beginning, God gave certain instructions to his people to follow. As long as they keep these in mind they will think twice about indulging in sinful activities.

It is the same way with parenting. When parents teach children about what is right and wrong, and consistently repeat it to them, they are more likely to grow up doing right all the time. The more they repeat the right things, the more they understand what the boundaries are, and less likely to indulge in sinful activities. The Bible is filled with scriptures that state walking the right path and doing what is right is instrumental in leading a sin free life. For example take Philippians 4:8:

"Finally brethren, whatever things are true, whatever things are pure, whatever things are just, whatever things are pure, whatever things are lovely, whatever things are of good report, if there is any virtue and if there is anything praiseworthy - meditate on these things".

The barriers in a person's mind are not something that can be felt or touched. This makes it difficult to see when something is going wrong. This is why it becomes easy to be manipulated. Because the barriers are invisible, forming a defense around it is difficult. Creating and following proper and straightforward defense methods is necessary to protecting oneself.

The will to do what is good and right is not an automatic one. The carnal mind would easily choose to do what is wrong. It is essential for everyone to constantly build right thought patterns and do what is necessary to ensure these thoughts are consistently maintained. Even God does not force anyone to do His will. He created each and everyone with a mind of their own.

No-one can make a person stay within their boundaries. It is something only the believer can do on his own. He may get encouragement from friends and family, but ultimately, it is his responsibility.

There are three enemies of the Christian - the world, the flesh, and the devil. They can totally destroy the barriers or subtly alter them and the believer will not be aware until it is too late. It is critical that when the believer has decisions to make, he keeps in mind what his barriers are.

CHAPTER 3

A MIND READING TRICK FOR A
LIFETIME OF SUCCESS

The mind is a powerful organ for reading and also for reasoning in the right way. But the mind does not just reason because it wishes to reason but sometimes is controlled by the individual. Of course when reading, the mind is totally concentrated to what is being read though sometimes the person may read without actual concentration, but this is this occurs rarely. Mind Reading trick is very crucial when an individual is interested not to deviate from what they are reading.

Most often, to achieve appropriate understanding from what is being read, it is good to have enough good rest. Rest is so important that without it a lot of things go wrong. The mind as a body organ for reading should be given enough rest before it can function properly. This even explains why the mind finds no difficulty concentrating in morning hours as compared to the afternoon session. This means in order to understand what is being read, it is good to have enough rest.

Besides it is always good to read what you find interesting and appealing. When you read something you lack interest in, it often leads to boredom and sometimes result to sleep in between studies. Reading topics of interests refreshes the brain again and again and can result to a healthy lifestyle all together.

Moreover, the mind acts in such a way that it concentrates better when there is a routine a routine to follow. For instance anyone who makes up their minds to study at a particular time of the day easily absorbs what is being read because the mind is programmed to absorb studies at that time. This is a general rule of the mind; it performs better when programmed to act in a certain way.

Nevertheless, to see to it that concentration of the mind is not so disrupted, it is imperative to avoid certain things such as drinking alcohol or even taking in hard drugs such as cocaine, heroin or 'weed'. These are dangerous drugs to the human mind and its functionality. These can distort your way of thinking.

Reading in tran□uility may also serve as prere□uisites to effective understanding of what is being read or studied. Usually □uite places can be freaky, therefore making an environment so conducive for learning is very important. Of course, most people find joy and happiness when studying in tran□uil atmospheres.

Sometime reading may be difficult not because of where an individual is reading from, on these occasion taking advantage of mind reading tricks can help an individual understand what they're studying.

A mind reading trick can easily be obtained if the one involved knows exactly what disrupts his or her when reading. That is why it is often good to know what the confounding factor is when it comes to your studies and finding solution to it. This is can be □uite easy if you know how to control your mind.

THE HUMAN MIND - WHAT'S YOUR CHOOSING?

If you had to chose between challenge and typical, what would you be your choosing if you only had 6 months to live? Your everyday average or, perhaps an experience that you have always dreamed or planned to do and is within your reach might be a likely answer. With experience, the ladder for such an answer would most often be not getting the average pooh-poohed rewards, gifts or the most desired results wanted for the time you are alive if you have such a deadline.

Being on numerous experiments in the last 3 years to keep growing ad getting educated on both sides of the ladder, there are heavy but interesting learning degrees for living the type of romantic cliches bestselling books teach and remind us. If you knew how much time you have left and it is only a couple years o months, you surely up your ante to do actions faster.

What happens if your deadline is shorter or longer? The good or bad spirits from the "guija" game might tell you, but guys like you and me might not be interested. So how you can easily chose an exciting lifestyle, day to day adventures and remembering experiences for generation to bloodline generation? Pretty interesting but yet simple, am I the right guy to answer it for you?

I can surely be a guide because of two main reasons. Have been in top of the world family wise and financially virtually for decades and have been in learning and challenging experiences as my own choosing to experience the ordinary lifestyle. Both are incredibly fulfilling, however, one road has better options in our today challenging world.

As a major purpose is starting to be fulfilled and being in both sides of the fences as a kid and in adult age, I would like to let you know or remind you of a very important truth. Thoughts lead to feelings, any kind of feelings lead to actions and your actions will definitely get you given result. That result for defining "living life to the fullest" will all depend on your vision and adapted social conditioning over the given years.

A social conditioning example is one you have

permanently selected or one partially exploring. Having deep needed studies on the human mind, I have personally discovered in great two additional great insights. Insights that no book can ever describe or paint the picture better than your actual viewable outline of it! Such being, rich people truly believe in creating their own destiny while poor people (a poor mind) would usually believe "life just happens to me!"

A top favorite heard numerous times among friendly get-togethers is in huge controversial comparisons. Needed to say in advance, boy will I probably get in heavy trouble by saying this, a masochist understanding for some but a fine tuning for controlling emotions in the highest available levels as one of my personal "getting stronger" skills as I write before going big in new projects. Let me tell you, Puerto Rico has the best conglomerates of nicest and biggest emotional souls, me being one of them. Some will probably punch me if I say it in their face!

What is the discovery? Have you ever heard people or even a friendly answer and even confirm you by arguing on interesting conversations "Joe, money isn't as important as love!" Now isn't that the most ridiculous and dumbest social conditioning thinking ever!

How about framing with the following so you may understand the hidden codes in such statement!

What's more important, your tongue or your ears?

Correct answer being, both are highly important! If you only had 6 months to live, 5 years to live or perhaps knew in advance that you only had 15 more years to live you know that money will be extremely important in the adventures you want to fulfill and unimportant in the most emotional haves such as, family if you and I were to think alike.

Whatever you end up choosing, make sure to explore and target fulfilling opportunities. Be it on your next vacation or your next move - make sure to ask yourself "Am I Living Life to the Fullest?" Plan and have fear as an ally and not as your biggest enemy.

Making sure to create our own bucket list, aiming and firing at will is a needed blessing! Get your bucket list together and greatly consider having such list fulfilled before the bucket kicks you. From experiences in my mid 20's, you can live a lifetime in a day(s) or just a handful of weeks. Make sure you set time for your own destiny. Your mind and your own judgment would be the most precious assets in creation for such fulfillment! Should be continued?

MANKIND'S FASCINATION WITH THE HUMAN MIND

Ever since mankind could ask the serious questions, he has pondered what makes the human mind tick? Why do we think the things we do? And thus philosophy has been able to capture the imagination in countless hours of thought.

Recently I met a young man and comments were very interesting indeed. He made a very telling statement after giving many excellent examples and a set of questions and observations worthy of merit about how the brain was able to do the things it does. And after pondering this all he admitted this to me in a brief statement when he wrote:

"It is something that has motivated me to completely change my plans for the future."

That is a powerful statement not only have philosophers throughout time spent many hours wrestling with all these thoughts, this gentleman of college age has decided to change his life plans and search for the answers. Powerful indeed; so I asked him;

"In what way have you changed your plans? Are indicating that you have a feeling that you should be doing something else with your life experience? And if so does it involve your interests of the human brain or mind? What might your line of study or research be leaning towards?"

ART AND ITS IMPACT ON THE HUMAN MIND

Many different forms of art have been shown to have profound effects on the human mind. Alzheimer's patients, for example, are often involved in music therapy, which has shown to help them recover and reconnect with past memories. Even if only momentarily, the memories they experience have shown to increase positive moods and improve their □uality of life.

Most forms of art are able to impact the human mind in one way or another, even if it may be negative. What is most important is to explore the impact art has on the human mind and figure out how to positively harness the impact and minimize any negativity.

Pop art, for example, impacts different people in different ways. With its strong ties to commercial consumerism and found art, it is easy to evoke emotion in someone when utilizing the properties of Pop art.

Nostalgic Undertones

Emotions and feelings surrounding past events can be easily conjured up through the study of Pop art. Pop art is specifically tied to nostalgic thoughts since many of these works utilize old comics, food wrappers, advertisements and other types of found art that people may recognize from past events in their lives. Many of the most famous pieces in the Pop art movement have utilized popular advertisements that could be easily tied to past memories.

Utilizing pop art to delve into past memories can be very therapeutic for many different reasons. For example, if someone is dealing with a childhood trauma, memories from childhood can help them figure out exactly what happened and how to move past it. Through art pieces that they can associate with their past, the memories will come more freely since they are not elicited by direct objects, but indirect thought instead.

Clearly art therapy can work in regards to bringing back past memories. Pop art is not the only type of art that can be used to help stimulate areas of the brain and help in the process of resolving issues.

The Brain Feels Rewarded

According to a 2010 study conducted by researchers at the Emory University School of Medicine, viewing paintings as opposed to photographs of similar objects evoked more of a sense of reward within the brain. Participants in the study were shown pieces from different artists such as Van Gogh and Picasso, and then they were showed photographs that depicted very similar objects. When they studied the brains of the participants through imaging technology, the ventrial striatum, which is part of the reward system, became more strongly activated when the participant saw a painting rather then a photograph of a similar object.

This area of the brain is typically tied to different types of addiction, especially gambling. With the power of art being able to affect the reward system in such a powerful way, it begs the question as to whether certain types of art may be able to help stimulate the brain in a way that helps with addictive behavior.

Benefits to Underprivileged Children

Art therapy has also been used to awaken the senses of underprivileged children through both the viewing and creating of art. According to research compiled and analyzed by Christina Pili, the experiences that disadvantaged children are often exposed to can create deep issues in regards to their motor, social and cognitive abilities. With these types of issues many children begin to develop nervousness, anxiety, sleeping excessive or too little, and a lack of verbal, social and language skills. Music, dance, painting and other forms of art have shown to have an incredibly significant and positive effect on children who come from disadvantaged homes and have been exhibiting delayed behaviors in these areas.

By awakening the senses through experimentation with the different types of art these children are experiencing, they are able to see increased abilities in their cognitive, motor and social skills. These are invaluable skills that are important to their overall quality of life.

The Many Colors of Pop Art

Returning one last time to the power of Pop art on the human mind, some studies show that different colors are able to tap into various emotions within different people. Pop art is known very well for its use of bright, vibrant colors. Bright yellows often evoke a feeling of happiness, which is a very common color in Pop art pieces. Depending on the color within the piece, different emotions can be displayed by the observer.

Clearly different aspects of art and the participation in the arts can have a profound and positive effect on the human mind. Pop art is especial useful in helping evoke past memories and gain insight through the use of bright colors. Art is a beautiful thing to be enjoyed, and knowing the powers it can have on the human mind is certainly an added bonus.

THE HUMAN MIND & WRITTEN WORDS

The brain is an amazing tool that is intensely complex. While reading is only one of the tremendous amounts of uses we have for the brain, it is a very important process, and the one we will be talking about in this article.

When we see and read text on a page, the information is comprehended by an area in the brain known as the Wernicke's Area is where the information is collected and translated into usable information. This area of the brain takes the information gathered from written or spoken language and passes the information along to other systems which then translate into motor actions.

This is very interesting because it is unsure how words can be stored as ideas and concepts. Most likely things are related to each other in the memories, therefore you can remember that a cat is a cat because of the combination of its looks, texture, color smell and other senses.

These concepts can be amazingly confusing, but the human brain works very well to comprehend all of these systems □uite smoothly.

There was a study done by Cambridge University that discovered that the human brain can comprehend words based on the location of the first and last letters while the center characters can be presented in a randomly mixed fashion. An example is as follows:

eevn toghuh this text cemos aocsrs as jmlbeud at a first gnalce it is acalutly quite easy to read, very aaznimg if I do say so melsyf.

This is possible because the human mind interprets words as a whole, not by each individual letter.

IGNORANCE AND THE HUMAN MIND

Although there are many subjects that we communicate about freely, there are some subjects that are generally classified as taboo or even forbidden. Speaking particular words or phrases in relevance - sometime not even upon these protested subjects, is wrong in what can only be described as a delicately instant mortification. This phenomenon needs clarification in part and is directly related to how the human mind works. Communication is a fundamental of all life.

If at this point you think I am referring to pornography or criminal acts then you are reading the wrong article.

Many terms of languages seek through the ages of progressive culmination to define as best possible a phenomenon or thing or activity. But terms are rarely one-sided - which is to say that there is a cause and an effect really going on, there isn't just one absolute.

Ignorance is a term that is an example of the effect term. The word is meant to describe the observed effect, which per the definition is "the state or fact of being ignorant; lack of knowledge, learning, information." What would be the cause term for this? It is confront - in this case no confront, defined as "5. to bring together for examination or comparison."

This is an example of the cause and effect terminology presented for our particular phenomenon. Usage and ambiguity of terms like this are a common example of the degrading effect the so called field of study - psychology, has had on education methods, technology and standards.

How do we increase our ability to confront?

Confront is one of the components of Communication. It is a necessity because it is required along with intention to impel what is being communicated to the destination.

Confront is increased by increasing familiarity.

Familiarity is gradient condition of a beings willingness to reach or withdraw from something.

So, if one is perfectly willing to reach for and also withdraw from something it is said to be very familiar. Familiarity is the primary condition for confront.

A specific process has been designed and trademarked called "Reach and Withdraw". It resolves familiarity to a high level so confront is achieved, not ignorance. Confront is essential to be able to handle or resolve a situation or problem. Confront is the primary condition to handling any problem.

Train a person's ability to confront and you create a person who handles things like it is their own without reserve or obsession. This clarification of some fundamentals related to communication and the function of the human mind are directly relevant to causativeness and effectiveness of a person. They are the foundation, that they can be improved is what is new.

WEALTH AND THE HUMAN MIND

"Money is not real, its just an idea." If this is actually true, and of course it is, how come many people all over the world are still broke? Simple. It is because they don't apply the simple principles of success, of which I will highlight for you.

If you will diligently apply these principles, those lovely ideas of yours that have been lying fallow for years, will turn into a gold mine for you.

1. Vision

When God gives you an idea, make sure you also receive a clear vision for that idea. An idea without a vision will not see the light of day. So, what is a vision? A vision is a goal or purpose/objective with a clear cut plan/strategy. Your idea must have a purpose and a strategy for implementing the idea.

2. Knowledge

Now you have got a vision/purpose with clear strategy for your idea, good. Add to your knowledge. Go for knowledge! Study materials that have connection with your idea voraciously! Learn from those who have used an idea similar to impact their World and return, pull in so much wealth. Remember, knowledge will not drop on your lap, you have to go for it! In our book, any body can do well in life, I talked extensively about the importance of knowledge. Go for knowledge with all diligence, and as you find it apply it to your idea and you will see results springing forth endlessly that you may not be able to contain.

3. Passion

Good, you can have some good Knowledge about your idea. Add to knowledge, passion! Be strongly attached to your idea. Think about your ideas all day long. Talk it, imagine it, feel it, act it. Let it consume you totally! Your passion needs to be so strong that you can even die for it. Have an innermost conviction about your passion such that people around you would definitely believe in you.

4. Discipline

A person with a great idea should expect all forms of distractions. You cannot afford to sacrifice your beautiful ideas on the alter of distraction. No way! So, to turn your ideas into money, you must be disciplined! Be so disciplined such that anybody who come into your world, would know what you stand for. Those ideas of yours must touch lives and bring you big time money, so, you cannot afford to be tossed around by all forms of trivialities!

And most of all you have to believe in yourself that the ideas, vision passion and discipline you have, that you have the ability to bring about that which you so desire to come to pass. Don't allow anything distract you from your vision and dreams. You must keep your focus again, again and again until you hit that target of yours. You must also dream big, so that when you achieve those dreams of yours, you don't end up being dissatisfied because your dreams were small. We all love you and encourage you to keep reading our articles because as you read, your life will never remain the same again. God bless you!

You have to believe in yourself that the ideas, vision passion and discipline you have, that you have the ability to bring about that which you so desire to come to pass. Don't allow anything distract you from your vision and dreams. You must keep your focus again, again and again until you hit that target of yours. You must also dream big, so that when you achieve those dreams of yours, you don't end up being dissatisfied because your dreams were small. We all love you and encourage you to keep reading our free downloadable articles at [http://www.one-word.org] because as you read, your life will never remain the same again. God bless you! Wealth And The Human Mind

"Money is not real, its just an idea." If this is actually true, and of course it is, how come many people all over the world are still broke? Simple. It is because they don't apply the simple principles of success, of which I will highlight for you.

If you will diligently apply these principles, those lovely ideas of yours that have been lying fallow for years, will turn into a gold mine for you.

1. Vision

When God gives you an idea, make sure you also receive a clear vision for that idea. An idea without a vision will not see the light of day. So, what is a vision? A vision is a goal or purpose/objective with a clear cut plan/strategy. Your idea must have a purpose and a strategy for implementing the idea.

2. Knowledge

Now you have got a vision/purpose with clear strategy for your idea, good. Add to your knowledge. Go for knowledge! Study materials that have connection with your idea voraciously! Learn from those who have used an idea similar to impact their World and return, pull in so much wealth. Remember, knowledge will not drop on your lap, you have to go for it! In our book, any body can do well in life, I talked extensively about the importance of knowledge. Go for knowledge with all diligence, and as you find it apply it to your idea and you will see results springing forth endlessly that you may not be able to contain.

3. Passion

Good, you can have some good Knowledge about your idea. Add to knowledge, passion! Be strongly attached to your idea. Think about your ideas all day long. Talk it, imagine it, feel it, act it. Let it consume you totally! Your passion needs to be so strong that you can even die for it. Have an innermost conviction about your passion such that people around you would definitely believe in you.

4. Discipline

A person with a great idea should expect all forms of distractions. You cannot afford to sacrifice your beautiful ideas on the alter of distraction. No way! So, to turn your ideas into money, you must be disciplined! Be so disciplined such that anybody who come into your world, would know what you stand for. Those ideas of yours must touch lives and bring you big time money, so, you cannot afford to be tossed around by all forms of trivialities!

And most of all you have to believe in yourself that the ideas, vision passion and discipline you have, that you have the ability to bring about that which you so desire to come to pass. Don't allow anything distract you from your vision and dreams. You must keep your focus again, again and again until you hit that target of yours. You must also dream big, so that when you achieve those dreams of yours, you don't end up being dissatisfied because your dreams were small. We all love you and encourage you to keep reading our articles because as you read, your life will never remain the same again. God bless you!

You have to believe in yourself that the ideas, vision passion and discipline you have, that you have the ability to bring about that which you so desire to come to pass. Don't allow anything distract you from your vision and dreams. You must keep your focus again, again and again until you hit that target of yours. You must also dream big, so that when you achieve those dreams of yours, you don't end up being dissatisfied because your dreams were small. We all love you and encourage you to keep reading our free downloadable articles at [http://www.one-word.org] because as you read, your life will never remain the same again. God bless you!

CHAPTER 4

MAPS OF THE HUMAN MIND

The human brain learns and orientates itself by forming mental maps of familiar places and situations. Similar to a physical map, these mental maps not only shows the perception of the maker, they form landscapes in their own rights.

"Looking at a map can teach us more with our eyes in an hour than we can learn from our ears in an entire day". This valuable insight was expressed in 1605 by the cartographer Thomas Fuller. By looking at a historical map, you will get an idea of how strongly a particular image of the world can determine people's thoughts and actions. For many thousands of years, most Europeans believe that the world was flat and therefore had no idea of the real position of the continents and the oceans in relation to one another. This conviction imposed considerable limitations on how far seafarers were willing to travel. It obviously hindered any endeavours for discovery. This was because people believed that they would fall off the edge of the Earth if they traveled far enough. They had a limited idea of the vast expanse of the oceans and the lands beyond the horizon.

Before sea adventurers could venture into new lands and uncharted seas, a new picture of the earth had to be thought of. Once this gained gradual acceptance, the speed with which exploration took place took off. Bit by bit, mile by nautical mile, the whole world gradually opened up to explorers and discoverers. If the Genoese seafarer Christopher Columbus (1451 to 1506) had not had the audacity and vision to imagine that the earth might be round, and that new land might be discovered by sailing westwards, sea exploration might have been held back by decades or centuries. Later generations of Europeans would have held on to the erroneous opinions that Asia was on the eastern part of the world and cold therefore only be reached by crossing the eastern oceans.

In our modern work life, we often use many expressions that show the significance of visual pointers for human action. For example, when your company has embarked on a marketing plan, you might say that you can "see what is wrong with our marketing strategy and decide on the next course of action". Quite often, it is very difficult to organise an action without having a mental picture of the result you wish to achieve. For example, if you have a problem, the solution to that problem comes easier if you can visualise it. Then you devise a map to find solution or routes to solve the problem or work around the problem. Similarly, mentalists who to achieve great feats of memory recall use mental maps to train their memory and improve their memory techni ues. Students have also been trained to use mental maps to improve memory, their study skills and accelerate their learning. They do this by breaking down course structure down to subjects, down to topics and down to detailed concepts or formulas, much like the a map of a city or town.

Basically, your mind think in pictures and having such mental paths help anyone from a busy executive, managers or marketing people to plan new campaign or product strategies. The paths make it easy to link a seemingly unrelated concepts or ideas to a bold new strategy or package an old product into something new using fresh ideas. With such mental maps, you use your ability to retrace paths in your mind and to store maps to your memory in a manner much more easier than you think.

So like the maritime maps of old, new frontiers are being discovered by understanding the natural way the brain thinks, stores information and solves problems. All made possible because mental maps frees the limitation of conventional human thinking.

OPENING THE MIND - HOW TO ACCESS THE SUBCONSCIOUS MIND

If you want to access the subconscious mind, it's easy. You just need to shut the conscious mind up.

The catch is, that's nearly impossible. The conscious mind is a huge part of our day. So huge, in fact, that we tend to think of our conscious mind as ourself.

It's not. If we were exactly e☐ual to our conscious mind, we'd cease to exist when asleep. Or dreaming. Or daydreaming. If we were our conscious mind and nothing more, we'd never have an intuition or a hunch or a gut feeling.

Brain scans of sleeping subjects have shown that in various stages of sleep, the brain can emit higher amplitude brainwaves than when awake, and even consume more oxygen than when awake. This means that our brains can be more active when we're unconscious than when we're conscious. There's more going on up there when we think there's nothing going on up there. And there's even more going on up there when we're not thinking at all.

Clearly there's more to me than my conscious thoughts.

The conscious mind is the thinker. The subconscious mind is the knower.

The conscious mind is a thinking tool. It really is like a train, a vehicle. It's meant to be used, not to be the user. As the sleeping/waking brain scans show, the conscious mind really is akin to the oft-□uoted tip of the iceberg, with the bulk of it, the subconscious mind, being below the water line.

When your conscious mind has run amuck, you'll be anxiously trying to figure out who you are and what you should do; you'll be trying to think yourself into being. When your conscious mind is stilled and your subconscious mind takes precedence, you'll know who you are, because your subconscious mind is the knower.

Descartes said, "I think, therefore I am." Cogito ergo sum. And since then, most modern people have eᐤuated the ability to reason as proof of their humanity. However, ancient scripture describes the revelation of divinity when God said, "I am who I am." Meaning that being is being, without reason. Reason comes from being, not the other way around. Existence just is. Mind cannot wrap itself around the fact of being because mind is a subset of being, and the subset cannot encompass the superset.

In order to know, thinking must cease. Not for

knowing simple facts like two plus two, but for knowing mysteries like the grandeur of a mountain range or the infinite depth of a night sky. And why these inspire some people to feelings of transcendence but yet others to feelings of annihilation. The rational mind can lead us to understand how brain chemistry comes into play, but it cannot lead us to know the experience of wonder itself, much less why the experience is important. It can conjecture, but it cannot truly know.

To ▢uiet the conscious mind and access the subconscious mind, we have to offend the conscious mind, interrupt it, ▢uiet it.

Why would I want to bypass my conscious mind to reprogram my subconscious?

First, because the subconscious mind is the real driver of action. Willpower can keep away a few cigarettes or a few extra servings of cake and ice cream, but eventually the subconscious has its way. This is what St Paul describes in Romans: "For the good that I would I do not: but the evil which I would not, that I do."

For real change to happen, the conscious and subconscious minds must be in alignment; so here are some practical principles to accessing the subconscious mind:

First, get plenty of sleep.

Studies reveal more and more that sleep is absolutely crucial to proper brain function. No longer dismissed as a waste of time and a weakness, sleep has been shown to be essential for processing memories, balancing body chemistry and cleaning the mind of negative emotions that have a detrimental effect on the whole person. Get plenty of sleep.

How much? Studies suggest anywhere from 7.5 to 10 hours. Your needs probably lie somewhere in between. Err on the side of more sleep. Imagine how much sleep you would be getting in a natural environment without artificial light. You'd go to sleep shortly after sundown. Suddenly, ten hours of sleep per night seems quite reasonable, doesn't it? That's how our ancestors would have slept, for millennia. Late-night culture is younger than Thomas Edison.

Waking Techniques

Waking techniques such as hypnosis and meditation are also helpful in □uieting the conscious mind. Here are three practices that you may find beneficial in □uieting your conscious noise, opening your mind and accessing your subconscious. These are practices that can be practiced for short periods daily or more often:

1. Meditation

The basis of meditation is to observe one's thoughts without judgement, without labelling them good or bad. Just to observe them as you would observe birds and bugs flying by your window.

Then you will realise that your thoughts are not you. Then you will feel comfortable detaching your sense of self from your driving thoughts. Then you will no longer be under the control of your thoughts but begin to control them.

Sit comfortably for twenty minutes without interruptions and just observe your thoughts - as though they were leaves floating by on a river; you pick them up, look at them with a goofy smile on your face and put them back down to float away.

2. Hypnosis

The basis of hypnosis is to enter a relaxed,

uncritical state where the conscious mind ceases its judgemental function. This is the hypnagogic state, where post-hypnotic suggestions can enter the subconscious mind.

For many, the idea of giving up critical control is frightening. This is because they've been brought up on cogito ergo sum. If I believe that I am my thoughts, the idea of giving up my thoughts is like suicide. At least, to the ego it feels very much like death. But it's not really death. It is just the quieting of a part of you, like slowing down your heart rate. As essential as your heart is to you, your heart is not you. As essential as the mind is to you, your mind is not you. There is more to you. And when the lesser can be quieted for a moment, the greater can emerge.

Related to hypnosis are various forms of subliminal programming. These range from audio tracks such as the famous stop-smoking tracks with affirmations exhorting you to quit smoking recorded beneath soothing music, to sophisticated Paraliminals, which are a fascinating technology using a simple stereo recording to play back one message into your right ear and another into your left ear, with increasing degrees of overlap.

The theory with Paraliminals is that the conscious mind overloads and gives up - here is the principle of pattern interrupt, of offending the conscious mind - leaving the subconscious mind to piece together the input. This results in the programming suggestions bypassing the gatekeeper, the conscious mind, and being accepted as truth by the knower, the subconscious mind.

To practice self-hypnosis, search online for an excellent hypnosis, subliminal or Paraliminal audio and listen to the guided hypnosis. They usually last from half an hour to an hour.

3. Brainwave Entrainment

Finally, there are the methods that seek to modify the mind by changing the brain.

When we're actively thinking and solving problems - or feeling anxious - our brain emits an electrical fre□uency that neurophysiology categorises as beta waves. In the hypnagogic state where we're open to suggestion and super learning, our brains emit alpha or theta waves. In deep sleep, delta waves. *

Modern brainwave entrainment methods, first developed in the 1930s, train the brain to function at specific bandwidths for short periods of time, exercising the brain to function more often in those states, namely the alpha, theta and delta states associated with relaxation, creativity and learning.

Ever been in a shopping mall when a familiar song came on and you found yourself tapping your foot and humming along without realising it? Brainwave entrainment audios use the same principle, but with much more precise frequencies.

Do a search for brainwave entrainment audios and spend some time with them every day. They're really enjoyable; I've tried a few and recommend The Morry Method.

Caution: Recordings that ☐uiet the conscious mind should not be listened to while driving, operating machinery or balancing your chequebook.

Is all this pseudoscience?

Compared to the realm of physiology, the field of psychology is more recently explored; and the area of human potential and the science of mind even more so. Thus, much of it may seem esoteric and unfamiliar. This is expected of any new field of endeavour.

Before we're through, some things will have been shown to have been pseudoscience while others will be proven legit. Already, the increasing overlap of neuroscience - traditionally a domain of physiology - into the field of psychology is proving rather gratifying.

One can sit back and wait till everything's settled, or one can roll up one's sleeves and dig in. Which way you decide will largely depend on your temperament and values.

Our conscious mind is the tip of the iceberg, and just a part of our being, like a vital organ. We are much more than our conscious mind; we are moved mostly by the unconscious mind that lies beneath the water line.

In order to open the mind and access the subconscious mind, we need only still and □uiet the conscious mind through daily habits that can be practised for twenty minutes or more at a time, namely:

- Meditation, which is to observe our thoughts and disidentify from them.

- Hypnosis, which is to bypass the critical, conscious mind.

- Brainwave entrainment, which is to train the brain to function habitually at alpha, theta and delta bandwidths.

LEARN HOW TO READ MINDS IN 72 HOURS OR LESS - USING ONLY A PAIR OF HEADPHONES AND YOUR PC

Who else wants to learn how to read minds? Think it's impossible? Think ESP, telekinesis and all sorts of psychic mind "tricks" are nothing but fantastic fantasy or fiction? Are you skeptical that clairvoyance and other amazing intuitive abilities are real? If you are anything like I once was...the simple truth is that you are probably VERY snobby about what you DO believe...and don't'! But the simple truth is that mind reading is not only an ability that many people possess...it's something you can learn to do 100% on your own. (and completely from home)

So what changed MY thinking about ESP and mind reading overall?

First....I read a lot about it. Then, I spoke to people who could DO it...and who demonstrated it on me! (and if you need proof...that's just about the BEST way I've found to get it..:-) Lastly...I learned how to become a mind reader myself, and while I'm NOT nearly (yet) as good as some of my mentors, and teachers, I'm getting pretty close...and can do all sorts of things that I never believed were possible at all. (let alone within the parameters of my own potential powers)

What is the FASTEST way to learn how to

mind read....without buying any courses or investing in any silly seminars?

Honestly? Binaural Beats, which are a safe, proven and foolproof technology for inducing PROFOUND altered states of consciousness are probably the very BEST way to open, and then EXPAND your awareness to tap into the consciousness of the universe...and then of course, into the thoughts of others.

Now, understand this:

I can't get into a whole dialogue in this short article about how mind reading works. There are actually lots of different theories...and I'm not sure which one I tend to believe is MOST accurate for me. But the general idea is, consciousness is something that permeates the universe. And our minds....are NOT located in our heads. (as in....your mind is NOT your brain) As a matter of fact, many very smart people believe your brain is more like a radio...or TV set. The SIGNAL is coming from outside of the TV (or radio) and the instruments only decodes that signal...and projects it so we can listen, or watch. Our brains act very similarly, reducing those signals so we can understand and interpret them...but actual CONSCIOUSNESS, is "out there", not in your head.

Why is that a significant point to understand?

Because when you use Binaural Beats, or brain entrainment technology as many people like to call it, you are actually EXPANDING your mental abilities by tapping into MORE of the information stored in the universe. And thoughts....as in the thoughts of other people, are ENERGY...and are stored in that same universal field. (scientists call this NON-LOCAL mind)

Sound confusing?

It's NOT..:-) And you have to experience it for yourself, to understand how completely life changing this experience, and information can be! The good news is you can now access this technology on your PC, and using nothing but a pair of headphones and a little commitment, you can have your first GENUINE mind reading experience in one weekend or less.......pretty much 100% guaranteed!

WHAT PROVOKES MENTAL ILLNESSES TO THE HUMAN MIND?

Mental illnesses are the result of psychological disturbances provoked to the human side of the human conscience by the anti-conscience.

The anti-conscience is the part of the human conscience that belongs to the wild side of the human brain. It occupies the biggest part of our brain, and it is too violent, evil, immoral and sneaky.

This is our primitive conscience, which is schizophrenic, because its development was totally disorganized and chaotic.

In order to be happy, the live conscience needs organization, understanding, compassion and patience before the difficulties of existence, otherwise it can only lose control when facing pain, becoming too violent and aggressive.

Our primitive conscience has to learn how to forgive and have pity on its enemies, but it is a cold and wild monster that refuses to study and that cannot feel anything.

The anti-conscience is very powerful, because it is too huge and it has too much energy, besides being able to think independently of the human side of our conscience.

It can completely destroy our human side by provoking dizziness, hallucinations, unbearable feelings and sensations, besides interfering in all our thoughts.

In order to discover its existence, I had to pass through too many unbearable experiences, after seriously studying the meaning of dreams and various scientific subjects for four years. And, after finally discovering its existence, I had to wait 19 years before being able to present my scientific conclusions to the world, after continuing the research of the psychiatrist Carl Jung into the unknown region of the human psyche through dream interpretation.

The anti-conscience is a true demon. It is the separate brain of a wild monster, which lives inside our brain, and influences our human side all the time. It is our wild and primitive personality, without any human consciousness, that is still alive and keeps trying to control our behavior.

It doesn't know the difference between what is

good and what is bad, and it is totally indifferent to moral rules.

Carl Jung couldn't see its existence, because he was afraid to continue the research in the human brain through dream interpretation, since he knew that craziness was hidden there, somewhere. He had discovered that it existed a priori inside the human brain, by observing the behavior of many patients who suffered from grave mental illnesses.

He thought that the unconscious mind was as evil as wise, even though this contradiction is totally absurd. Evilness is poison, while wisdom is medicine. Both are incompatible.

The unconscious mind that produces our dreams is only saintly and wise. Another part of the human brain has the evil characteristics that Jung had observed: the wild side of the human brain, which provokes all the existent mental illnesses to the human side, in order to destroy it and take its place, completely controlling our behavior.

I had to delay so much in order to reveal to the world my discoveries, because this reality is too tragic. I had to give to the world the solution at the same time as revealing the tragic truth; otherwise it would provoke panic in the population.

The tragic truth is that the anti-conscience is too powerful and this is why it usually destroys a very big portion of our tiny and under-developed human conscience through mental illnesses, even when it doesn't manage to destroy it completely.

The miraculous solution for us is the translation of the meaning of our dreams, since the unconscious mind produces them in order to give us directions, so that we may learn how to transform the terrible anti-conscience into a positive, intelligent and talented part of our human side, eliminating forever its evilness and absurdity from our minds.

CHAPTER 5

HOW TO READ FACES & PROFIT

Yes, you can profit from reading their faces. And you can prove it to yourself. Remember, every face reveals its personality and destiny.

Use the nine descriptions below. Stop and think about how and where you can use this information.

1. A ROUND FACE SHAPE loves people, food, and small talk.

2. FLAT & CONNECTED EYEBROWS are free thinkers and can be very jealous.

3. EYES WITH LARGE IRISES are emotional and close to their family.

4. HOOK NOSES handle money very well, are thrifty, and skeptical.

5. A FLARED (wide at bottom) GROOVE (under the nose) has a lot of sexual energy and capable of producing many children.

6. The FULL LIPS is generous, affectionate, and likes to talk.

7. A CLEFT CHIN is passionate, playful, and affectionate.

8. PROTRUDING EARS are non-conformists, possessive and will have early success.

9. 2 VERTICAL WINKLES BETWEEN THE NOSE indicate a planner, thinker, doer.

Did your uses include; sales, relationships,

looking for a partner, communications, counseling, job interviews, family, friends, boss, co-workers?

STUDYING THE EFFECTS OF HOW THE MIND REACTS TO STORIES - A VIABLE PURSUIT INDEED

Think about this for a moment, it's true that humans take stories seriously, and it is amazing how tales foretold tend to stick in the memory. It's also interesting how stories over the generations evolve and meld with the culture, shaping it, and holding it together. Nations, religions, cultures, all held together by what - stories, tales, and narratives. Amazing isn't it? So, it makes a lot of sense that we ought to study this.

For instance consider the challenges we have in education, corporate training, or even keeping people working together for the common cause of our society or civilization? Stories help, they help break the ice, they help for comic relief, they help say things that are often difficult, but telling something through a story - well it works doesn't it? Thus, we ought to use stories as much as possible.

The piece went on to add; "they change the course of insurgencies, frame negotiations, play a role in political radicalization, influence the methods and goals of violent social movements, and likely play a role in clinical conditions important to the military such as post-traumatic stress disorder."

Wow, see those points? Now then, let's switch gears here and let me tell you a though I had for this rather intriguing DARPA project about storytelling. I have some thoughts I'd like to share with you, okay so, here is the idea; The human voice box rattles or gives off a change in vibrational frequency when someone is of a very strong belief on the topic they are discussing.

This happens in business with branding, with devoted religious folks, or with anyone telling a story they truly believe in. It also has a way of coming out in writing, where folks can feel the emotional content. Perhaps someone like Steve Jobs or a fast mover in the political scene can do the same, perhaps a reverend or religious leader, and I bet this can be simulated by laying multiple tracks over speeches or instructional videos too.

I am somewhat sensitive to these vibrations, and I note my mind taking interest when these 'rattling vibrations' occur in other's voices, in fact, I am of no-religion, but when a devout person starts their spiel about their "religious wakening" or born-again moment, I find my mind shifting gears as if operating on a secondary brain wave.

Interestingly enough, I also note my own voice rattles, as I am very solid in my beliefs of such things as free-market capitalism, country, winning, and my company. When I am, I see people stop and take notice, as if I've captured them for a moment to insert my view points and vision. So, I think there is something to it, and it would stand to reason based on such historical things like "pipe-organ music" in churches and their vibrational fre□uency and the large number of enthralled followers.

Although, I've never read anything explaining all this, I feel there is something more here, something that could explain why stories "capture our imagination" and perhaps why we even use the word "capture" in the first place, see that point.

Questions:

1.) Have some humans, through gene expression, evolved to have stronger voice box vibrational ability?

2.) Can humans through practice hone this vibrational ability in their voices.

3.) Would practiced singers be able to do this? Is that why church's get large numbers to join their choirs?

4.) Does bowing and praying in the Muslim world cause shock waves to move forward and back during the rocking motion of praying, as savants often rock back and forth, thus triggering memory inducing brain waves?

5.) Does human passion cause certain chemicals in the body to react in engaging vocal cords? It would stand to reason.

6.) Did this ability help in the coming together of human troops, tribes, groups, communities, nationalities, cultures, religions, countries, movements?

Yes, well, as you can see, I have so many ⬜uestions on all this and speculations, and theories, if you are also intrigued by this, maybe we should talk? You see, I am a writer (hobby writer), and have this storytelling ability apparently, which served me well in business, sales, marketing, and branding. It's also been good to me as a writer. So, maybe we can help reform education, train folks better, allow for better memory uptake, and then, move the ball forward by doing what comes natural for human learning, and socialization.

In fact, I think this could be tested, simulated, and we could even use what we learn to mellow out problematic societies and rogue regimes that threaten the life-experience of human populations. Interesting isn't it? Yes, all of it is, so please consider this and think on it.

NUMENTA REVEALS THE SECRETS OF HUMAN MIND

Numenta, this is the name that has given Jeff Hawkins, one of the greater world-wide experts of artificial intelligence, to its last entrepreneurial idea. The objective of the plan is to lead searches on the operation of the human mind, trying to understand it through the use of information and communication technologies (ICT). "When you are born, you do not know nothing". With this phrase the American engineer has launched with enthusiasm its personal challenge to the understanding of the brain, emphasizing like, according to him, "to the birth our mind is similar to one blank sheet".

And it adds: "In truth some slight knowledge is known base, as an example is known like suck". But the point is that the brain, to the beginning, does not have some effective perception or vision of the world and the surrounding objects. "no knowledge of languages, houses, automobiles and computer", explains, churning the hand in order to mean the truth in its complex. "the brain must still discover that things of the sort exist. For me ", he underlines," it is a fascinating concept ".

An interest so strongly that it has pushed him to found an agency not profit, the Redwood Neuroscience Institute, and to enlist some of the most important student of neuroscience because they succeeded in to elaborate one unified cognitive theory.

The same interest that has finally lead it to the

creation of Numenta. Here, with its collaborator of long date Woman Dubinsky and others twelve engineers, are successful to develop a program of artificial intelligence that must be considered like the first software really based on the mechanisms operated in the human mind.

As the human brain, the software is born without knowing nothing. And like the brain, it learns from what it feels, building a model of the world, and makes forecasts on the base of this model. The result, explains Hawkins, is a thinking machine able to resolving problems that to the man can seem elementary but that in past they have always put in difficulty the computers, included, as an example, the sight and the movement. "The philosophical" woven of the activities of the company is constituted from the theories that the same Hawkins has collected and detailed in the book "On intelligence: how to new understanding of the brain will lead to the creation of truly intelligent machines "written in 2004 with Sandra Blakeslee.

The text crosses several disciplines of neurological and cognitive sciences and explores the possibilities that their study can be arranged with that one of the computing. From this union therefore, Numenta will try to draw as an example of the cues for the planning of innovative, applicable technologies in the systems of vocal acknowledgment in the within of the telephony services, as also in the systems increasing the visual abilities and also in the process control of industrial automation.

But Hawkins goes also beyond, prefiguring the possible developments of Numenta. In fact is convinced that its program, equipped of a power and highest speeds of elaboration guaranteed from use of digital processors, is also able to resolve complex problems facing them with the same ways of the mind of a child, that is perceiving them like a flow of new data to read. Is sufficient to enter the obtained information from a net electrical worker in the system and Numenta derives a virtual model that represent how the net works. And just as a child succeeds to understand that a glass thrown on the pavement breaks off itself, therefore the system learns in which cases this is possible. Between some year, it supports Hawkins, these systems will be able to capture anomalies and trend of whichever truth, from the securities market to the weather one, with a today inconceivable reliability for the computers.

UNDERSTANDING THE SUBCONSCIOUS MIND - A CRUCIAL STEP IN MAKING LASTING AND MEANINGFUL CHANGE

Everyday, people from all over the world read or listen to what the Law of Attraction gurus have to say. They then proceed to get all pumped up and excited about all the wonderful changes they're about to make in their lives, and then, after a few days or weeks, perhaps even months, they ultimately resort back to their old ways of thinking and doing. They don't see any immediate changes in their lives, so they slowly start to lose focus and/or faith in what they've learned and fall right back into their old habits. Does this sound familiar? It's not that what they've learned is wrong. It's just that it is not complete. In order to be successful at making major changes in our lives, it is critical that we first understand how our minds work.

Think of the conscious mind as a laptop computer, with limited memory and processing power. Through your laptop (conscious mind), you can install programs or issue commands to control most of your bodily functions based on data that you observe or experience at any given moment.

The subconscious mind, on the other hand, is like a supercomputer or server, with all of your human instinctual behaviours pre-programmed at birth and everything you've ever experienced through any of your five senses stored away in it's massive memory banks for safe-keeping. On it, is but one program (or operating system), and for every piece of data (or experience) it processes, a corresponding set of commands (reactions) is issued to the body based upon all of its stored data. It is this supercomputer that maintains control over all of your bodily functions 24 hours a day, 7 days a week, over the course of your entire lifetime. That is, unless, it receives an overriding command issued through your laptop computer (conscious mind). Also, it is only through your supercomputer (subconscious) that you are able to access the Internet (or Universal Mind) through which all other supercomputers are connected and accessible to each other.

Scientific studies have demonstrated that once a fact is known by at least one person, it can then be accessed by the subconscious minds of others, thus supporting this Universal Mind theory. Understanding how the human mind works and how to gain access to it, enables us to then ac□uire this knowledge from the subconscious minds of others by way of our sixth sense, intuition.

For hundreds of years, everyone believed that it was impossible for a human being to run a four-minute mile, until, of course, Roger Bannister figured out a way to do so. Within the next few years, 24 other runners were able to accomplish this same, previously unfathomable feat. Could this be considered further evidence supporting a Universal Mind theory?

Anyway, back to our computer analogy; even though our conscious minds (laptops) do have some control over our bodies, it is still our subconscious (supercomputer) that maintains control whenever our conscious mind is overwhelmed with data (sensory experiences) or shuts down completely (sleeps). So, what little control our conscious minds have, will always be handed back over to our subconscious when we become distracted (new input), overwhelmed (too much input) or go to sleep (power down). Hence, in order to make lasting changes in your life, you must:

1) never lose focus or become distracted (highly unlikely),

2) never be overwhelmed (impossible), or

3) find a way to modify your supercomputer's operating system (ie. make changes to your subconscious mind)

This is what so few people appear to be able to do successfully. In order to reprogram your subconscious mind, you have to find a way to override years and years of learned behaviours and somehow impress a powerful enough message that it will take precedence over all of these automated behaviours and responses. In essence, you will have to find a way to program new lines of instruction or code into the subconscious' operating system that will have the ability to override potentially thousands of lines of existing code in order to achieve your desired outcome (response). Can it be done? Absolutely, but the process is definitely more complex than simply reading a few books or repeating a set of positive affirmations.

There are actually several ways of getting through to our subconscious, and now that we have a basic understanding of how our mind(s) work, we can proceed to exploring the various methods available for incorporating meaningful and lasting changes for the better. This is the key to designing a better life. We must find a way to modify our deepest beliefs about ourselves.

THE POWER OF THE UNCONSCIOUS MIND

The power of the unconscious mind is tremendous, even in healing the most serious of diseases.

Cancer--the word alone strikes fear into the hearts of many who have seen it ravaging the body and life of a loved one--can be healed. Sadly, the incredible power of the human mind to heal the body, is largely overlooked in research.

Fortunately, holistic health care pioneers are

making progress in rectifying this oversight. For instance, Dr. Rob van Overbruggen's research has allowed him to identify many of the psychological patterns that

influence the cancer process. Louise Hay's research identifies the mental causes for physical illness and the metaphysical way to overcome them. This valuable research is the culmination of these author's many years of extensive research, and their recognized expertise in Hypnotherapy, Neuro Linguistic Programming (NLP), and Time Line Therapy.

American Health Magazine reported these findings from a comparison study.

o Psychoanalysis: Creates a 38% recovery after 600 sessions

o Behavior Therapy: Creates a 72% recovery after 22 sessions

o Hypnosis: Creates a 93% recovery after 6 sessions

Hypnosis is a dynamic and vital healing process embracing all aspects of health care. Hypnosis is client-centered with its focus on the discovery of the origin of a person's issues. Through the process of hypnosis/regression the unconscious mind goes to the original cause, which then gives the person and practitioner the opportunity to process the original feelings surrounding the original experience/cause. These surrounding feelings can be healed, thus empowering the person to live the life they want to live.

This study confirms--Hypnosis is more effective and works more quickly than traditional talk-therapy or psychoanalysis. In a hypnotic state, you are more receptive to new ideas and you can more effectively process the emotions linked to the experiences, which created pain, fear, sadness, anger, guilt, shame, humiliation and low self-esteem.

Through Hypnosis you connect with your

subconscious mind, which puts YOU in control of your subconscious mind--the most powerful and empowering aspect of your brain.

THE EVOLUTION OF MARKETING - CONNECTING BEHAVIOR WITH THE SUBCONSCIOUS MIND

An evolution is currently taking place in the field of marketing. This evolution has to do with the exponentially increasing understanding of the human mind - the subtle yet profound influence of the subconscious mind on human behavior.

Conscious awareness is merely the beginning of the journey into the mind. Neuroscientists agree the vast majority of cognitive processing takes place outside of conscious awareness. Most neuroscientists estimate between 90-95% of mental and emotional activity occur outside our conscious notice. Much of this "underground" activity is automatic and emotional. Much of this commotion is bubbling just below the level of our awareness.

So what's the fuss? Why care about mental activity that goes on behind the scenes?

The main reason is that subconscious activity has a massive impact on our perception of the world, daily behaviors, buying decisions, and satisfaction with life.

For example, the price of wine influences how people perceive the same bottle of wine. When people are told the price of wine is higher, they subconsciously create the perception of a better tasting wine. The "higher priced" wine is perceived to have better, more desirable characteristics such as improved body, taste, and aroma in comparison to a glass of the same wine with a reported "lower price."

Another study showed that brand recognition plays a large role at the subconscious level in influencing how we perceive objects, such as soda. Blind taste tests may show that individuals like drink A over drink B by a large percentage. However, when those same individuals can see the product packaging and brand, they prefer B by a wide margin. No change in the two drinks, just an awareness of the brand which subtly yet powerfully kicks the subconscious mind into motion and changes the way the taste buds perceive drink A compared to drink B.

In addition, conscious self report measures such as polls, surveys and focus groups are poor predictors of consumer behavior. Self report measures are notoriously flawed in their ability to predict future behavior. The relationship between what consumers intend to do and what they actually do is low and can be completely unrelated at times. For instance, over 60% of individuals who tested a new kitchen appliance in their home stated they were "likely" or "very likely" to buy it within three months. Nearly a year later, not even 13% of those consumers actually followed through with their stated intention and bought the appliance. In following up with those who said they were going to buy but did not, it was discovered that this group could not explain the disconnect between their stated intention and their behavior.

What's more, the subconscious mind works at lightning fast speed. It works so quickly that it can pick up information from the environment that does not even register in the conscious mind. For example, a message which appears for a brief 30 milliseconds (below the temporal threshold of conscious awareness) dramatically affects individuals' behavior in the near future. An automobile manufacturer tested a new sensor system which automatically measured the speed of the car as well as the distance of an object directly in the path of the car. When the program discerned a high probability of a crash, it flashed a message on the windshield, "Brake!" During testing of the program, it was found that the ideal length of time to flash the message on the windshield was 30 milliseconds - so fast that the conscious mind was not even aware of it, but the subconscious mind was. When the message was shown for 30 milliseconds, drivers demonstrated optimum braking ability. When the message was displayed for longer periods of time (so the conscious mind could "see" it), the braking performance of drivers declined.

These examples are just the beginning of a revolution in marketing, advertising, branding, and improved consumer experiences.

With the birth of new imaging tools and innovative methodologies such as Resonance Technology's approach to get at passionate feelings, the mind is rapidly beginning to reveal its secrets. Similar to exploring the deepest depths of the ocean, we are on the verge of stunning new discoveries. And, among others, marketing and branding professionals stand poised to reap the benefits.

CHAPTER 6

BENEFITS OF THE MIND CONTROL METHOD MEDITATIONS - 7 REASONS WHY YOU SHOULD MEDITATE

Mind Control meditation is a worldwide recognized holistic discipline during which the practitioner trains his or her mind in order to realize some benefits.

The benefits of meditation have been

scientifically proven by many researches. The Time Magazine even devoted an entire issue to Meditation and credited it as a solution to a wide range of illnesses from skin conditions, stress, and chronic heart disease to AIDS and infertility. It even reported that "meditation can sometimes be used to replace Viagra".

So, what positive change can you bring to your health through the

1. Relaxation

No stress More and more studies are linking stress as a common factor to many diseases and everyday illness. Knowing that our stress levels effect our health, it's good to know how to reduce stress and induce relaxation in our daily life.

Meditation based on the Mind Control method plays a huge role in stress and relaxation. It helps to clear ones mind and encourages you to live in the present. When you live in the present, rather than the future or the past, relaxation naturally occurs.

2. Sleep Better and Learn to Practice Creative Dreaming

Silva Mind Control improves sleep Whether you have troubles falling asleep or just simply can't sleep (does the word insomnia ring a bell?) then meditation is a healthy and effective alternative to over the counter medication.

The simple act of meditating calms the mind and induces relaxation and a relaxed mind and body are key to achieving a good nights rest. Similar to how our body releases chemicals when a fight of flight (or a stressful) situation is induced, our body also releases chemicals when we meditate. The chemical released via meditation is known as serotonin. Why does this chemical matter? Studies have concluded that individuals suffering from insomnia have low levels of serotonin. Meditation helps to naturally raise serotonin levels and the chances of insomnia occurring greatly reduces.

The method teaches you to "command" your mind to let you fall asleep when you choose to. It also shows you how to set your internal clock to be able to wake up anytime-without the use of an alarm clock! Just imagine how much productivity and energy you will gain by always having a good night's rest. The possibilities are endless!

3. Stop bad habits

Quit smoking Many people smoke when they're stressed out, overwhelmed or simply out of habit. Silva Mind Control classes can help you (or your loved ones) to quit smoking because they focus on reducing stress and promote a healthy state of mind.

Deep breathing calms the mind and helps to rid the body of unnecessary stress. The less stress, the less likely the chance to reach for that cigarette. And even if the thought of smoking crosses the mind, meditation induces a healthy state of mind so the chances of turning to that cigarette is reduced. The mind is naturally more calm and present and the chances of making the proper decision (not smoking) increases 10 fold.

4. Learn Faster, Remember Better, Improve Grades

Use meditation to learn faster Mind Control techni□ue has been proven to raise IQ and to boost memory.

In a study conducted by the Autonomous University of Tlaxcala in Mexico, it was found that 67.7% of university students improved their IQ classification after using the Silva Mind Control Method.

5. Develop Your Creativity

Improve creativity Studies show that creativity is enhanced when functioning at the Alpha level.

Listening to the Mind Control exercises, you will learn how to enter the Alpha level on command and then to use your creative mind to help you think of solutions to problems, enhance creativity or let inspiration flow.

Silva grads have used this process to develop patents, start new businesses, or to create works of art, literature and music.

6. Think Big and Attain Powerful Goals

Find your life purpose With Mind Control, you will experience life changing moments WITHIN the modules themselves. Sudden bursts of creativity, coincidences, health improvements, flashes of intuition-these combine to alter your belief system.

Studies have shown that the Mind Control programs lead to you becoming more self-assured, positive, healthy and most of all, they help you learn how to think bigger, set higher goals and seek to achieve things that contribute to humanity.

7. Develop Intuition

Discover your hidden potential A research project conduct by Dr. George Maycock at Appalachian State University in North Carolina demonstrated that students who completed the Silva training showed a significant increase in creativity and intuitive functioning. Of the 30 students who participated, 25 showed gains in intuitive abilities.

Four of the other five (who did not show improvement) were already functioning in a high intuitive mode before the training. Intuition is valuable for students- and for adults too. One researcher found that 70 percent of gifted or high-IQ students were predominantly intuitive, while only 39% of students in regular classes were intuitive.

HOW TO ATTRACT MONEY USING MIND POWER

While I cannot claim to be wealthy, and am still in the process of learning what constitutes a life of abundance, as a massage therapist and naturalist I am blessed with work that is fulfilling and provides me with the means to meet my needs.

There are several aspects to consider when thinking about financial freedom; including these questions: what are the ethics of socio-economics, what are we thinking, and what are we doing?

Throughout history, we find that every culture has deities in charge of money, wealth and abundance. Prayers and offerings are made, temples built to appeal to higher powers for wealth and abundance. In the Judaic-Christian Bible, the Book of Job depicts the story of a man devoted to God, who despite leading an honorable life following the religious practices of his time, nevertheless suffers loss and heartache. Who hasn't wondered why some seem born to fortune, or lucky, while others are desperately poor?

In an effort to answer these ⬚uestions, I have often turned to the teachings of a number of teachers who have devoted their time and efforts to helping others to realize their greatest potential. In the following paragraphs, I discuss the work of several inspirational authors and teachers who have been mentors to me and my family.

Patricia Cota-Robles is a New Age inspirational

author and spiritual teacher, founder of the non-profit, educational organization, New Age Study of Humanity's Purpose. Her approach to abundance is from a very spiritual perspective, and yet re□uires incisive personal assessment and practical steps that need to be taken. In her book and CD, "Abundance", Cota-Robles suggests a number of affirmations and prayers. What is uni□ue about these affirmations is that they include expressions of love, forgiveness and gratitude. Through the Gift of Prosperity, "the substance of money becomes tangibly available and flows continually into the hands and use of every life-stream, organization or activity that is receiving the ideas from the Divine Mind of God to restore this Planet to Her Diving Heritage which is Heaven on Earth"

In Patricia Cota-Robles' book "Abundance", she says that in order to realize financial freedom, it is necessary first to clear our relationship with money. Feelings of fear and confusion come from childhood programming, misunderstandings, and sometimes even the often-held religious belief that poverty and suffering is somehow a path to spiritual growth.

Low self-esteem and unworthiness also contribute to negative thinking that confuses our relationship with money and interferes with our dreams of financial freedom.

Cota-Robles counsels the time-honored tradition of tithing, explaining that there is a second, very important factor in attaining financial freedom. According to the laws of the Universe, there must be a balance; we must give something back. Very important in this interaction is that we give with the feeling of gratitude for the gifts that have been given, as she explains, "giving our money away in loving gratitude for our gift of life."

The idea of giving back and including re□uests for the same blessings for others in prayers and affirmations for money is often a missing element in many self-help and wealth consciousness books and programs.

Another inspirational author and teacher that

has been a mentor for me is Wayne Dyer. He has a number of books and CD's on self-realization. His latest may be one of his best. He says, "The greatest gift you have been given is the gift of your imagination. Everything that now exists was once imagined. And everything that will ever exist must first be imagined."

Wishes Fulfilled; Mastering the Art of Manifesting - by Wayne W. Dyer

Make no mistake however; Wayne Dyer's method is more than just sticking positive sayings on the bathroom mirror (although I say to use any method that works to kill our ANTS or Automatic Negative Thoughts as Dr. Daniel G. Amen calls them). Like all the truly effective practices, there must be physical, applied practice. Wayne Dyer teaches the practice of training the imagination, practicing the art of assuming the feeling of wishes fulfilled, and practicing with steadfast resolution. Sakyong Miphan Rinpoche, author of the book, Turning the Mind Into an Ally", likens our untrained mind to a wild horse.

James Allen, British philosopher, inspirational writer and author of the well-known book "As a Man Thinketh", wrote, "Through his thoughts, man holds the key to every situation and contains within himself that transforming, regenerative agency by which he may make of himself what he wills."

Think and Grow Rich by Napoleon Hill

Think and Grow Rich is the book that started it all. While today there are any number of books and programs on success, the power of the mind, and how to manifest our dreams. This book was a groundbreaker in the self-help, motivation and inspiration movement. Written in 1937 during the Great Depression, Napoleon Hill's book "Think and Grow Rich" is still one of the most influential and widely read motivational books on success. Over 70 years later, it is currently ranked by Business Week

Magazine as the sixth best-selling paperback business book. Napoleon Hill explained that the philosophy outlined in his book not only will help a person develop material security, but also will help people to succeed in almost any endeavor.

In his book "Think and Grow Rich" Napoleon Hill outlines the thirteen principles (originally there were sixteen principles), founded on his earlier work "The Laws of Success". The earlier work was the result of over twenty years of research with the cooperation with over 500high-achieving, wealthy and successful individuals. The thirteen steps discussed in the book, with accompanying case studies and examples, are:

Desire

Faith

Autosuggestions

Specialized Knowledge

Imagination

Organized Planning

Decision

Persistence

Power of the Master Mind

The Mystery of Transmutation

The Subconscious Mind

The Brain

The Sixth Sense

HELPING TO UNDERSTAND BODY LANGUAGE
RE: LYING, DATING AND JOB INTERVIEWS

Your body language says a lot about you and has a major impact on how others see you. As such you can learn a lot from the body language of others.

Body language accounts for up to 55% of how

we communicate. Body language along with verbal cues can indicate a number of different things depending on the context. People with powerful body language with open movements that take up more space tend to feel more confident. They are more likely to have less stress, be more dominant, take more risks and be more optimistic. Dominant body language creates a powerful appearance. Studies show that even faking high and low poses effected the confidence level of the participants both positively and negatively.

The idea of fake it til you make it may seem false, but in faking it the process will help you become it starting with small changes to your body language. Something everyone can learn.

Here are three common situations in which body language is especially important - a job interview, dating and detecting lies, and ways to read between the lines to help understand what is really going on.

Like it or not we all lie a lot. When conversing with a stranger we are likely to lie once or more in the first 10 minutes. They may be little lies but we still do it. Most of us will participate in deception from time to time to avoid conflict, but we are probably better off telling the truth. Words can be deceptive but the human body has a hard time hiding lies. Using your own body language and being able to read body language of others can be extremely useful when communicating with others.

The Basics of Body Language:

Your primary goal when reading body language is to determine their comfort level in their current situation. There is a process of combining verbal cues and body language to determine this.

Positive body language:

Moving or leaning closer to you

Relaxed, uncrossed limbs

Long periods of eye contact

Looking down and away out of shyness

Genuine Smiles

Negative body language:

Moving or leaning away from you

Crossed arms or legs

Looking away to the side

Feet pointed away from you, or towards an exit

Rubbing/scratching their nose, eyes, or the back of their neck

A single cue can be misleading so it's essential to pay attention to multiple behavioral cues.

LYING:

Being able to judge whether someone is lying through reading their Body Language is a big advantage. Your intuition is never 100% accurate, but with practice you can become more aware of when you're being lied to. This techni□ue will help with the big lies but it's very difficult to detect white lies, lies of omission or exaggeration.

Research has shown that liars often exhibit much of the uncomfortable behavior plus some specific additional traits.

Fake Smiles

Research has shown it is almost impossible to fake a genuine smile when lying. This is why many people appear awkward in family photos. The smiles look awkward if they are faking it. Your genuine smile is in the eyes as your smile pushes up your cheeks and creates wrinkles around your eyes. It is difficult to fake this as you need to feel some genuine happy emotion to do it and that is almost impossible if you are lying. So a fake smile is helpful in determining if a lie is in progress.

Too much Eye Contact and a Stiff Upper Body

Often a liar will overcompensate with too much eye contact, and appear stiff while they try not to fidget, this can make you feel uncomfortable and unsettled. In genuine conversations people move and do not hold eye contact for long periods. Liars because they are uncomfortable will often rub their neck or eyes and look away to the side and opt to do little. If you notice tense shoulders and a high amount of eye contact you likely talking to a liar..

Verbal Cues

Pay attention to the conversation, liars will offer more details and suggest punishments for the real offenders if they are being accused of something. They will answer your ⬚uestions with a question giving them time to make up an answer. This type of conversation paired with negative body language points to dishonesty.

It's important to realize that some people may always behave awkwardly. Look for multiple cues and trust your instincts and ask for verification if you just aren't sure.

DATING:

On the first date understanding your date's body language is incredibly helpful in knowing when not to talk about something that makes them uncomfortable.

Basically you are just looking for general indications of comfort and discomfort. This means paying attention to how guarded their body language is. On a first date most people will be fairly guarded crossing their arms, keeping a distance and keeping their palms face upwards. Your goal is to encourage them to be more open by being more open and welcoming yourself with uncrossed arms and a warm genuine smile. We all tend to mimic the behavior of others so if you're warm and comfortable it will help them become more comfortable.

Comfort levels can fluctuate on a first date as they are nerve-wracking, and you are likely to make a few mistakes. Don't worry just keep going. Watch for positive body language and focus on what brings that out. If you witness negative body language change the subject. Of course there will be evenings when you just don't jibe with the other person and there will be many awkward periods. If this happens know that person wasn't for you and move on.

JOB INTERVIEWS:

Job interviews are similar to first dates except

that on a date you are on an e☐ual basis whereas in a job interview the interviewer has the power. This creates a situation were you are more uncomfortable than the interviewer. You could easily display negative body language which you need to override in order not to appear closed off.

First Impressions

First impressions do count so a smile, a handshake and a warm greeting along with the previously mentioned positive body language will bode you well for a comfortable interview.

Go into the interview prepared, this will increase your comfort level and add to your confidence level. To prepare research the company and any individuals that may be interviewing you.

Natural comfort is your most valuable tool,

however there some tricks to help you enhance your comfort. Eye contact is important especially when asking ☐uestions and when the interviewer has something to tell you. Avoid blocking your eyes, lean slightly forward, and appear to be a good listener by placing your hand over your mouth indicating you are not going to talk and are paying attention.

Any reasonable Interviewer will understand that you are a little nervous and tense. In fact if you're overconfident it can indicate that you are not taking the interview seriously.

Understanding body language along with verbal cues can be useful in communicating and understanding others. It can be fun, but you're not a psychic, you can't read minds or interpret what someone is thinking or feeling. Use these techniques to find clues to help you understand other people and communicate better.

BETRAYED BY BODY LANGUAGE (EVEN WHEN YOU ARE TELLING THE TRUTH)

If you have read anything about body language, the chances are you have heard that 90% of communication is non-verbal. The actual origin of this slightly distorted statistic is the research of Dr. Albert Mehrabian who concluded in his 1971 study Silent Messages that communication in every conversation is 7% words, 38% sound of voice and 55% facial expression. Consequently, the 90% (or rather 93%) of all communication is body language is born. However, it would be wrong to assume that the majority of communication is made through body language. In everyday life, we don't usually negate what people say, so what becomes interesting about body language and how body language become useful is in relation to what is being said.

For patients with advanced dementia, phsyical appearance is a significant factor in the assessment of pain because of the reduced ability for verbal communication, but in almost other cases a nurse would not rely on how a patient is acting to suggest how much pain a patient is in, they would ask the patient. Similarly, if someone is sitting with their arms and legs crossed and has an annoyed look on their face, you are probably not going to talk to them. In this case, body language is 100% of the communication, but the only way to make sure is to speak to them. Body language betrays you by exposing your feelings and attitude, yet it is your words and their relation to your body language that are truly central to your communication.

Despite the importance of body language in communication, without the verbal part of the communication, non-verbal communication is ☐uite limited. It is the combination of words and body language that betrays you, especially when what you say and how you act do not match. Mehrabian labelled congruence or consistency between body language and words to be a crucial element of the study of non-verbal communication; looking for when a person's words and actions do or do not match.

But surely if a person hasn't studied body language you have nothing to worry about? Before there were books on body language, people were picking up on the signs without being total aware of what they were picking up on. When someone says they are happy but don't act happy, you aren't going to need a book on body language to help you read the signs. Even if the person you have been talking has not read the books, it is highly likely that your body language will betray you.

As you venture out into your day to day dealings with other people, what you need to be concerned with is not how you act, but how you act in relation to what you say. Your body language can be all erratic and excited if you are saying excited things, but, if you act erratic when you are lying, the situation is different.

But, if you are telling the truth, why would you want to fake body language? The answer is simply that we are only human. When we say nice things to our partners or talk to our bosses, sometimes we are just too tired or just not interested. We can be talking about the one thing that we think is the most interesting or exciting thing in the world, but if we are hungry, or tired, or ill, or just having a bad day, the words we use might be enthusiastic but our body language will betray us.

How do you fake it? Most experts say you can't fake body language. This is good news if you have read 'top ten signs she likes you' or 'how to tell if he is lying.' But if you are trying to make yourself look good then, this could be a problem.

So what do we do? The simple answer is we increase the incongruence between what we say and our body language. We increase incongruence in two ways:

This first thing we can do is be honest. Don't try to sound too enthusiastic if you are not. If you are feeling tired don't try and compensate by being overly excited. You can be excited, but don't over do it. If you disagree with someone don't lie to them. As much as possible, merely avoid directly answering them. So, when your girlfriend or friend asks "Do I look fat in this?" respond with a "You look great" or "You look good in that dress" and then try to change the subject. Whether you say yes or no, you are probably lying. So don't answer the ☐uestion. Don't avoid the subject, but don't directly answer the ☐uestion.

The second thing we can do is to be aware of how you are acting and do something different. Congruence is about continuity, if you cast doubt on the continuity of the signs, you should be able to make reading them difficult and so disrupt congruence.

Although telling the truth can be a delicate business, disrupting the congruence of your body language will re☐uire you to think about how you are feeling and to know a little something about body language. It doesn't require a great deal of information, but you should be aware that body language is usually considered to function in clusters, so what you are doing with your arms is only relevant if it relates to the expression on your face and how you are standing. When you need to ensure someone is not reading everything about you from your body language, you will want to break down the clusters of your actions and consequently disrupt congruence.

Areas of body language to focus on:

Facial expressions: if you are feeling bored then show interest, if you are happy show a little sadness, if you have nothing to say make like you want to say something. When whoever you are speaking to gives you the opportunity to speak and you don't, they will begin to □uestion their own understanding of you.

Eye contact: the failure to maintain eye contact

shows lack of interest or deception. Aggressively maintained eye contact displays a desire to dominate another person. Judge your own feelings and intentions and adjust eye contact accordingly.

Touch: attraction is displayed by physical touch. In a dating situation, if a woman begins to touch, however innocently, another person, she is showing interest in them. Avoid inappropriate touching. In the workplace, inappropriate touching is anything more than a handshake. Do touch in interpersonal relationships. You might feel tried, but your partner will really appreciate that hug.

Arms and legs: your posture betrays all kinds of things about you. Two elements to be aware of are pointing arms and legs and the open or closed body posture. Often we show interest in someone by pointing our arms and legs towards them. If we are not interested and ready to go, we may point our limbs towards the door in an effort to be ready when it really is time to go.

On a very basic level the open or closed body posture is the difference between crossed arms and legs and uncrossed arms and legs. The closed body says "I am not interested or listening." An open body says the opposite.

Tone of voice: how do you speak normally? Are you a loud fast talker, a slow quite speaker? Think about how you sound when you are angry. Don't get too carried away. You don't want the boss to think you are aggressive when you are just tired, but do think about volume, speed, tone and infusing your voice with a little emotion.

Your body language is going to betray you. An uncontrollable incongruence between how you are acting and what you are saying is going say something you don't want it to. Think about what you want to say and how you feel, and then do something else entirely. A little disruption goes a long way.

Disrupting body language can be hard work and is not something you would want to do all the time. If you use it regularly on an unusually perceptive friend, they will pick up on your signals and see through your strategy. If you disrupt congruence when you are feeling uncertain, you can fight back against the betrayal of body language.

LEARN HOW TO BECOME A MENTALIST - HOW TO READ MINDS IN 3 SIMPLE STEPS

People who know how to read minds are the envy of everybody. They can amaze anyone and instantly become the life of the party. They can also use their skills to make sound decisions, anticipate reactions and make life generally more pleasant for themselves. The good news is... you too can learn how to become a mentalist.

You don't have to go through too much hullabaloo to develop mind reading tricks and skills. Just by reading these tips below, you can learn how to become a mentalist in no time.

1) Ask the right □uestions.

If you want to know how to read minds, you can start by asking the right □uestions. These □uestions won't give you what you want to know directly. However, you would be able to figure out more or less where a person stands.

For example, you want to know whether a person is pro-environment or pro-capitalism. Ask them a □uestion that tackles both concepts. Ask about what he thinks of animals in a zoo and animals in the wilderness. Or you can also ask whether they recycle or not. If you want to learn how to become a mentalist, you have to know how to do your detective work subtly.

2) Look for clues.

There's always a clue to every mystery. If you want to learn how to become a mentalist, you have to start recognizing clues for what they are and connect them all together.

Let's say you're a wife who wants to go out with your husband tonight. Look at his face, the way he carries himself and his overall appearance. Does he look haggard? Has he brought home a suitcase filled with documents? Judging by the clues presented to you, you can already deduce how your spouse is going to react to your plans.

3) Follow the routine.

You may not notice it, but most people tend to be predictable. They usually follow the same routine day in and day out.

Betty, for example, likes to stop by the department store after work. If you have worked with Betty or have known her for quite some time, you should already be familiar with her after work excursions. And yet when you tell her that you know she's going to head to the mall after work, she's still undeniably surprised at how you can read her mind!

Why don't you try observing your own habits and see just how predictable some of your actions are? Doing this will definitely improve your awareness of other people's actions as well.

CHAPTER 7

THE POWER OF CONVERSATIONAL HYPNOSIS - LEARN HOW TO READ PEOPLE

Do you know why conversational hypnosis is talked about so much? Because with the help of this techni☐ue, you can secretly hypnotize people and your subjects will never even get a whiff of it! Sounds great, doesn't it?

But hold on, before you start hypnotizing

people conversationally, know that you need to be able to read people before you can go ahead with this process.

What is reading people with Conversational Hypnosis?

To put it very simply, it means sizing people up by studying their body language. You have to interpret the non-verbal signals sent out by people consciously or unconsciously by looking at them.

And then you have to correctly draw the inference as to what these people are like, what they might be thinking or what their inner universe is like without explicitly articulating your silent actions.

Other than studying body language, you can read people and understand their motives by keeping a silent vigil on their physiological change. Great and cunning actors can fake their body language or control or tweak around their body language, but you can never fake or control your physiology as our subconscious mind controls our physiology.

When you can read and judge people, you can understand or guess whether people are trying to cheat you or not, whether there is disconnect or not. In fact, you can look upon conversational hypnosis as a human lie detector.

The Power of Conversational Hypnosis - How Does It Help You Read People?

You can read and judge people by studying eye movements, whether they are going red or not, change in breathing patterns, the fre□uency of blinking, the pupil relation etc. You should even study the eyes and people's pollster.

Do you know by observing the signs and body

language, you can pick up clues and judge people whereas other people will fail completely to judge that same person?

In fact, things can reach such proportions that people may even think you possess psychic abilities! You just have to make full use of all the powers of conversational hypnosis.

The good news is this skill can easily be learned by anyone with the right training. When you know how to read people you can then respond with the right influences at the right time and the possibilities are endless.

TIPS FOR READING PEOPLE'S THOUGHTS

To Read the Thoughts

The idea of reading the thoughts of other people, has been one of those things that has been a topic of discussion for many years. Indeed reading other people's thoughts is one of those things that everyone has encountered many times during life. Many times you may have been thinking about a close friend or a loved one, and the next thing is that they call you on the phone or visit you. It could be easy to call things like this coincidence but if we consider that there may be more to this universe than meets the eye. So what is the truth about reading other people's thoughts? And is it possible to read the thoughts of another person?

The Power of Communication

It has been said that when you speak, the words only communicate a small percentage of the information. Some of the more important aspects are tone of the voice and body language. Indeed the tone of a persons voice and body language can show when someone is lying. Have you noticed when a person is lying they find it hard to make eye contact, so this points to the fact that spoken communication is not the only way that we communicate. Have you looked at the way that birds fly in perfect formation even though we do not perceive them communicating. So do we have the ability to communicate on a psychic level? And could it be the case that we all have the capacity to communicate on a psychic level?

What Can We Learn From The Near Death Experience?

There was a story of a man who had a near death experience when he was 16 years of age, but had an interesting story about his experience. Following the event he appeared to become more psychic, so when people asked him how did he become psychic he gave this answer. He said that you do not become psychic, you are psychic and you choose to forget you are psychic to make this earth experience more realistic. So could this suggest that we may have the ability to communicate using thought communication, and is this a skill that we can develop? And perhaps we may even be able to develop this by using methods like meditation. I have personally found that I have been able to pick up vague thoughts from my children following meditation. So does psychic abilities have links to the ability to read the thoughts of other people.

Good Relationships

It has been found that when people are in close harmony they tend to pick up the thoughts that each other is thinking, this tends to suggest the importance of having a good and close positive relationship. In N L P the suggestion is that by exercises such as matching breathing two people are able to build rapport. So the idea of reading the mind of another person could possibly be initiated by some form of mental permission giving. If this is the case then the idea of reading the thoughts of another person may be associated with the building of trusted relationships. So have you experienced thinking about a close friend and then being contacted by them, and have you found that a close friend has been thinking the same thought that you have been thinking. - Thoughts To Make You Think.

READ YOUR BOSS NOW - 3 WAYS TO READ HIS MIND

Who does not want to read his boss's mind? If you want to know how to read his mind, then this piece of information is for you.

Nature has given us a gift to actually read minds. The subconscious mind has powers that are beyond the conscious mind. By understanding the mind and how it reacts to situations, you will be able to learn how to decode the messages people transmit non-verbally.

You can actually learn a lot from one people by merely observing him. Follow these three tips to read the minds of others.

The Shifts in Voice

When relaxed, most people have a steady voice. If you have noticed a slight change in pitch or rhythm or the speaker's voice suddenly cracks, then you better be careful. There is something fishy going on.

False Smiles

Smiles can be very insincere and dangerous. The false smiles are easy to distinguish. To spot a false smile, they usually vanish immediately. The truthful ones fade gradually.

Gestures and Talk Mismatch

If the boss has gestures that do not match what he is saying, then you better trust your instinct. This means he is not sincere with his statements. For example, if he said you did a good job but points at you after he said that ⬜uite delayed, then he might trying to cover something.

There are countless ways to read your boss's mind. When he tries to act differently, like maybe when he is too friendly or too aloof, you should be alert at possible changes ahead. Good luck and I hope you put these 3 tips into good use in dealing with your superiors.

HOW TO READ THE MIND OF YOUR PROSPECTS

The answer is very simple, just ask "what do want from me?" It is one of those things that many people leave out of their business and then wonder "hey, what happened to my business?" Most of us don't give a darn about what our prospect wants. If we have to became a leader then we should always ask for feedback and it is that negative feedback which is more useful to us than the positive feedback.

At the end of the day, it is about results and if we continuously ask our prospects what they want from us then that is the start of us being separated from the most of the people out there because we as a marketer have started to go into the mind of our prospects by giving them what they want. This will add value to our trainings and teachings and will be appreciated by our followers.

So the first step to read the mind of our prospects is to Google Survey Monkey and register there. Here after getting registered we can create surveys with the help of easy to use templates and can send them to our followers and await a response from them. When we get a response from people we can sense a pattern as people tend to ask about some particular things over and over again.

This thing can be very powerful in trainings and seminars as you already know what people may ask. So by stepping into your prospect's shoes you are laying the foundation for being a leader who helps other people add value to their lives.

DOES YOUR EX STILL LIKE YOU? HOW TO READ THEIR MIND!

Arguments take place only when two people are involved. You cannot produce sounds with one hand. Same is the case with any relationship. Both the parties play their part in a break up. After break up, you may be interested in a come back but what is important is, is the other person eＱually interested in the reunion? This intention may not be stated directly but few simple tips can help you read the mind of your ex.

Know your welfare: Did he every try to find out your welfare? When the other person is not interested any more in the relation, he does not bother to call you. If not immediately after the break up, your ex should call you to enＱuire about your welfare. This is a positive sign for reunion.

Gather information: Does your ex gather information about you through your friends. Does he try to know whom you are seeing or meeting after the break up. There could be several reasons as to why he is gathering information. One reason could be that he still cares for you and is missing you. His ego may be preventing him/her from calling you directly.

You still meet: Do you still meet each other as fre□uently as you did before your break up? If not together, do you find him in a party, friends place, get together or even movies. This means that your ex still wants to be with you but is hesitating to ask you directly.

Still single: Even after your break up, your ex is still single. You do not find him going out with new people or making new friends. One reason may be that he has not found anyone as interesting as you are or someone who could replace you.

From these above hints it is clearly evident that you both still stand a chance for reunion. So do not waste any time and take initiate your first step towards reunion.

DOES MY PARTNER REALLY LOVE ME? 3 MIND BLOWING WAYS TO READ THEIR MIND AND FIND OUT THE TRUTH

Love is indeed no easy task for any one. For most people this involves a very tedious and painful task of trying to win your partner's heart. Emotions are a very complex process and the more you think upon it, the more things seem to be going the wrong way. Many a times in life we are baffled about the sincerity of love that our partner shares for us. Our mind boggles us with endless questions which seem to make things worse as each day passes by. Now, you can address your concerns and find out for yourself whether your partner really love you or not.

You may need to analyze the behavior of your partner towards you. It may take you some time to realize how to do this but make simple notes of how he/she takes care of your concerns. Does your partner care for you when you are hurt? Do they miss you when you stay away from them for a long time? Does your partner feel the same way for you as you do for them?

Second, find out how your partner responds to your efforts to make them feel warm towards yourself. How do they utilize their private moments with you? Do you see a spark in their eyes when you share such intimate moments? Does he feel bored to spend time with you now?

Finally, find out how much your partner is ready to go out of their way to make your life happy? For most partners, as time passes by, the bond grows stronger. They are ready to take a step always ahead in life to make you feel more comfortable with them. Does you partner give you that special feeling? If yes, worry no further. Your life is still the bed of roses that you always wished for.

MARRIAGE PROBLEMS - YOUR SPOUSE CAN READ YOUR MIND WHEN YOUR MIND IS NEGATIVE

Most marriage therapists and relationship books warn against "mind-reading," which means assuming that your partner knows what you want. With some couples this is good advice. But one of the reasons that marriage counseling usually fails in relationships with chronic resentment, anger, or emotional abuse is that your partner can read your mind when your mind is negative.

If you think or feel "nag, jerk, selfish, liar, loser, irrational, irresponsible, narcissist, borderline, or abuser" or make any other negative attribution in proximity to an intimate partner, it will certainly be communicated, no matter how positive the words you use; indeed, even if you say nothing at all. Remember, our species communicated sentiment through body language and emotional demeanor long before the development of language. Even low-grade resentment and anger -- irritability, impatience, defensiveness, chilliness, agitation, annoyance, and contemptuousness -- are clearly communicated without words.

All of this means that if you try to communicate verbally without changing how you think and feel, you will seem to people you love to be saying one thing and thinking another, which will make you seem manipulative, if not dishonest. You will almost certainly get a defensive or otherwise negative response, even if your words are entirely positive.

In contrast, getting in touch with your core value changes the way you see yourself and the people you love. It makes you focus on what is more important to you, connection or punishment, compassion or resentment, growth or the status-quo.

At the very least, activating your core value before you attempt to communicate allows you to be more authentic with loved ones and reduces the chances of a negative response from them. But even if it fails to improve your interaction, you will feel more confident and genuine within yourself by remaining true to your deepest values.

Many times the futile negative thought-positive talk dance reflects a superficial communication-skills approach to what is really a walking-on-eggshells problem, coming from chronic resentment, anger, emotional abuse, or verbal abuse. One sure sign that you are walking on eggshells in your relationship is feeling as if you're losing yourself in a stream of self-doubt. If that is the case it is even more important that you remain true to your deepest values. Authenticity comes from fidelity to your deepest values, not from indulging transitory feelings.

CHAPTER 8

IS THERE ANY WAY TO TELL IF A MAN HAS HAD THOUGHTS OF YOU ROMANTICALLY? LEARN HOW TO READ HIS MIND

Men find it difficult to express their feelings and hide behind the tough façade without revealing much. This does not mean they are devoid of feelings, in fact they are emotional too like women but cover it up with ease. Signs to pick up to know if he thinks of you romantically can be many, read on.

He is happy around you

Do you see him smiling a lot in your company? People are happy to be with someone they like, so if you see his smile reaching his eyes and his face lightening up with joy when you are around, then surely he is romantically interested in you.

He focuses on you in a crowd

There may be number of people present but he can see only you and no else and he trains his eyes on you this shows that he likes you and is attracted to you. He gives you his undivided attention and listens with interest when you speak

He might ask about you

He may take his friends help to know all about you, what you do and things that interests you. Or he may take a direct approach and talk to you to know things about you because he finds you attractive enough to stir up his interest.

He shows great interest in you

You may be in a group but he is interested in only you and has no qualms if others notice this. He may choose to come and sit beside you and engage you in intimate conversation, getting a little personal showing his romantic inclinations as far as you are concerned.

He wants to get physically close

As he chats up with you he may just put his arms around your shoulder or just touch you to make his point. His thoughts are romantically inclined which shows as he wants to get physically close to you.

He makes plans to spend time together

He may ask you to come for a movie or a day's outing as he is eager to spend time with you. He wants to know all about you and show that he can be an interesting company and may want to impress you.

His priorities have changed

Where once he would never let go of his time with his friends or never miss a game of soccer, now he happily lets go of these activities just to be with you. This change in his priority shows how deep his thoughts are for you.

HOW TO TELL IF A GIRL IS ATTRACTED TO YOU? 4 SURE FIRE SIGNS WHICH WILL HELP YOU READ HER MIND

We all know that women aren't too direct about the way they feel about guys therefore chances of them approaching you directly and letting you know the way they truly feel about you is next to none.

Therefore in order to figure out whether a girl truly likes you or not...You will have to pay close attention towards her body language and a few other special clues which most guys normally tend to miss.

Read on to discover what these signs are and how you can easily figure out whether a girl truly likes you or not.

She is very direct with personal ☐uestions...

If a girl is very straight forward with her ☐uestions and ends up asking you a lot of personal questions such as whether you are single or not...What sort of girls do you prefer etc etc. Then it's overly obvious that she is trying to figure out whether you are available for her or not.

Which obviously means she likes you and wants to know whether the road is open for her or not.

Is she laughing at your jokes...Even when they don't seem that funny?...

This is another very common thing which tends to happen in case the girl truly likes you. The reason why she shows extra emotions around you and ends up laughing at jokes which aren't even that funny means that she is trying get in your good books and wants to get noticed.

This also means that she is just trying extra hard to impress you.

Is she getting physically close to you while talking?...

Is she standing extra close to you while you are talking to her? A lot of girls aren't too comfortable getting physically close to a guy early on...But in case she is standing real close to you while talking then it's a clear sign that she has something for you.

Also in case she touches you while talking which may include...A tap on the shoulder or brushing her arm against yours again and again...It means she likes you and is giving you strong physical signs.

Is she paying too much attention towards you & ignoring everyone else?...

This is another thing which would happen in case a girl seems to like you. Do you get a feeling that she is paying extra attention towards you even when you two are standing in a group of people?

Does it seem like you are the centre of all her focus and she is somewhat ignoring the whole group? You see this clearly proves that she is giving you that extra bit of attention solely because she is into you.

HOW TO KNOW IF A GUY WILL ASK YOU OUT OR NOT? SURE FIRE TRICKS TO READ HIS MIND INSTANTLY

Sometimes, it's hard to draw that fine line between a guy just wanting to make a good conversation and a guy who likes you a lot. If women were created to be vocal about how they feel and what they think, men were created to be the opposite. So, if he just doesn't say much, how can you tell if he wants to ask you out?

Perhaps the first □uestion is, why do you need to know? Naturally, knowing someone likes you and wants to date you is an instant morale booster. But more importantly, a guy lobbying around but not seeming to ask you outright may need some encouragement from you. However, before you give him back the right signals, first you should make sure you're interpreting his correctly. Here are the tell-tale signs he wants to ask you out.

His body language gives him away

Notice the posture of interest. He leans towards you a little and makes sure he's facing you when he's talking. He looks into your eyes every chance he gets, and tries to hold this gaze. Notice how he smiles a lot, at you.

His nerves are all over the place

If he just wants to be friends, then he wouldn't be breaking into a sweat. But a guy who likes you and wants to ask you out will have cold, clammy hands and will start sweating when talking to you even though the air conditioning unit's in full blast. If you're observant, you may notice him fidgeting or trembling, and trying really hard to act normal despite it all. He may look away when you stare back, and will have that nervous laughter when he's attempting to hide those nerves.

He singles you out

He doesn't talk to you when you're with your gal pals, although it's obvious he looks your way. He only approaches you when you're alone, and when he can talk to you without other people listening. Notice how he tries to catch you eye in the crowd. He's silently telling you to move away from your friends, so he can talk to you.

His friends are acting up

If his friends know he's into you, they may turn completely ☐uiet, or may burst into a riot whenever you're around. They may start to tease him, or even you. If his friends are rowdy, don't take it as a point against him. They're simply telling you they have a friend who is so into you, but can't make a move.

He talks less, asks more

A guy who is into you will want to get to know you better. Notice how you answer a ☐uestion, and he's throwing another one right back at you. Although this may seem flattering, it will also be encouraging to ask him a few getting-to-know ☐uestions if you want him to ask you out already.

Pay attention to his hands

He may seem extra touchy, punching you lightly on the arm or touching your hand. Don't interpret it immediately as a sign of freshness. It's all his efforts to conceal nerves.

He builds you up

He will compliment your eyes, or your dress. He will want to agree with everything you say, and will try to sing you praises without making him look too patronizing. Help him out by finding something to compliment him about. This will up his self-esteem and get him ready to ask you out.

He finds common ground.

A guy who likes you will want to be in sync with your interests, so he knows how to ask you out. If you tell him you're into art galleries, he may say he likes art too, and that there's a gallery he's always wanted to see. And you know the rest.

HOW TO KNOW IF A GUY LIKES YOU OR NOT - 7 SURE FIRE TRICKS TO READ HIS MIND ALMOST INSTANTLY

They say real men are men of few words. Their actions do the talking for them, and on those rare occasions when they actually speak, the words they utter are deeply meant. Whether this is true or not, the opposite sex is often misled by how men show, and react to certain emotions.

Society has dictated women to wait for a man to make the first move, so many women end up guessing, and second-guessing a guy's actions and words. And even if the modern gal does put a brave foot forward to ask a guy out, she would still have to read his signs to know whether he's interested or not. The challenge begins when women have absolutely no clue as to what guys mean when they act certain ways. Here are some truths about men, and how to know when they are hooked.

1. He may stare, or avoid your eyes altogether

A guy who's into you would do anything to stare into your pretty eyes, because it's his way of letting you know he's interesting. But then, when you look back, his nerves start to get all jittery, and he has to look away. It's a little known fact that people who can look at others straight in the eye are sincere and honest, but cut the guy some slack. He's probably still as apprehensive as you are.

2. In a sea of people and familiar faces, he seems to see only you

At a party, does he seem to always seem to be "accidentally" bumping into you? Do you turn around, and catch him in the corner of your eye, looking at you and wanting your attention? He probably hasn't said it out loud yet, but when a guy no longer notices the long legs and beautiful faces around him, and gets tunnel-vision around you, he definitely likes you.

3. He gets flustered and may stammer when talking to you

He wants to make a good impression, but he's not quite sure what to say. You wouldn't believe the number of times he's rehearsed his hello.

4. He pays more attention to you during a conversation, and asks ☐uestions instead of talking about himself

When he actually talks to you, watch his ability to converse. Notice how your guy friends will actually have the tendency to talk about themselves, therefore boring you to death. But a guy who really likes you will put you first. He will ask ☐uestions that will get you talking, and will react empathetically to everything you say. A mistake many men make is when they become too patronizing, but it's probably a way to make a girl see that they're on her side.

5. He's always the knight ready to rescue the damsel in distress

Why is he always so willing to drive you home? Why does he always seem to offer to help you out? This is a giveaway. While other guys would rather play their PSPs and watch baseball on TV with their guy friends, this guy will be catering to your every whim. You may not even notice it. He may start small - carrying your stuff for you, holding a door for you, pulling a chair for you to sit on, etc. Suddenly he's a perfect gentleman.

6. He gets you sweet nothings, just because

This is a giveaway, and once he starts spending on you, you know he's really interested. Flowers? Chocolates? Cute little stuffed bears? Surprise lunch? There's nothing more to say to that.

7. Final clue. His friends act funny when you're around

We reveal everything to our girl friends, and so do guys. They let their friends know who they're crushing on, and that's why you'll see his friends nudging each other, fidgeting, or simply teasing him about you. There you go. Wait and see, and let the magic of love make a move.

HOW TO KNOW IF A GIRL IS READY TO BE KISSED OR NOT? IT'S ABSOLUTELY IMPORTANT TO READ HER MIND

Men and women speak different languages. You have to understand that your knowledge of a girl's hot buttons and intimacy issues can backfire on you at anytime because girls are unpredictable creatures. The way to make the most of your knowledge is to recognize what sensitivities are triggered at different situations.

In other words, it's a hit or miss thing. It takes experience to be able to determine when a girl is ready to be kissed or not. To get some clarity, look at the examples translating to female readiness.

Another glass of wine? Agree and drink up because she is more than ready to hook up after dinner and a few more drinks. But if you offer another round of drinks and she begs off then you're not going to score. Try again next time.

Looks matter. Women get prepped and ready for a date they actually like. If she shows up in jeans and t-shirt on your first dinner date, you better find another woman to entice. But if she shows looking like one hot number, that's a whole different ball game for you.

The whole experience is a good indicator, too. Looks can only go so far. By looks we mean the hair, clothes and shoes. You need to identify other factors when you meet your date. See how she speaks, the tone of her voice and everything else from her natural smell to the perfume she wears to the lotion she uses. If they all make you feel good then trust it. She must be ready for something other than dinner and drinks.

Eye contact. Very few people have the ability to make eye contact. So long as she's making eye contact while you're talking means she's entranced. You don't need to study to tell that a woman who locks eyes with you is ready for more intense and personal bond.

Her Attention. The way she gives you her 100% attention is a good indicator that she's interested. You might have been to some dates wherein the girls were more interested in the people around you. So you should know when your date has only eyes for you. It speaks volumes and you should be able to hear this. Otherwise, you're letting one good chance pass you by.

If she fumbles or takes her sweet time getting her keys from her bag while you walk her to her door means only one thing. She's waiting to be kissed. You've seen this move in movies.

If she touches you way too much. Touch communicates everything from rejection and fear to intimacy and willingness.

How to Analyze People

CHAPTER 9

HOW TO DO A POWERFUL MIND READING TRICK THAT WILL SHOCK ANYONE

The best mind reading tricks are □uick and direct. This trick is very simple to perform but has a remarkable effect on people. Without any nonsense, you just read their minds.

How It Looks To The Audience

The magician asks a spectator to place a silver coin and a copper coin on the table in front of him. The magician then turns his back towards the spectator and tells him to move the coins around, so the magician cannot know the positions of the coins.

He then asks the spectator to cover each coin with one of his hands. One hand covers one coin and the other hand covers the other coin. The magician then tells him to touch his forehead with one hand and place his other hand in his pocket.

The magician then instructs him to take his hand out of his pocket and place it over the copper coin. He then tells him to place the hand that was touching his forehead over the silver coin.

The magician turns round and emphasizes that there is no way he could know which hand is covering which coin. He asks the spectator to silently visualize which coin is under which hand. Slowly and dramatically, the magician announces which coin is under which hand - and he is correct!

The magician repeats the trick and is correct again.

How The Trick Is Done

The secret is simple. The hand that was covering the silver coin is the hand that was touching his forehead. Because he was touching his forehead, there will be less blood in this hand and this will make the skin color lighter in appearance. So, you just quickly compare his hands when he is covering the coins. The hand that looks lighter in color will be the one covering the silver coin.

However, the key here is that you just have a

uick glance at his hands and then pay no further attention to them. You want to create the impression that you are reading his mind - not staring at his hands.

The method is helped by the fact that after you initially ask him to touch his forehead, you ask him to place his other hand in his pocket. Then you ask him to cover the copper coin with the hand that was in his pocket. This confuses the issue and helps to put the spectator off the track from guessing the secret. It also ensures that his other hand will be held to his head for as long as possible.

The only thing you will have to be careful of when performing this trick is using someone who has a suntan. If the person has a deep tan, then it can be more difficult to detect the change in skin color. So, do not use anyone who has a tan. Keep to pale skins.

FUTURE INVENTIONS - MIND READING CYCLING HELMETS

With all the intelligent inventions that are have been introduced to us over the past few years it comes as no surprise when something new is invented and changes the way we live. It is becoming harder and harder to shock people with new and interesting creations, with the wide range of innovative products now on the market. It is amazing what some companies are coming up with and this next invention may just take you by surprise.

According to research, you can now buy a helmet suitable for bike riding that actually reads your mind. This sounds like a bizarre and untrue story but the product is real and has been created by a top bicycle manufacturer. It has now been revealed that this protective headwear will not only process your thoughts but can also be used to control your bike.

The manufacturer has created a uni☐ue kind of

headgear that can be connected to your bike and controlled by your very own mind. It has a number of metal sensors attached to the inside which make contact with your scalp and these sensors then read your thoughts, are transmitted down into the bike and the action then takes place.

The bike incorporates a smart phone attached to the handlebars, this monitors your heart rate and the speed of the bike, and also receives the transmissions from the helmet which connects to the bikes gear system. Changing gears can now be done all through the power of thoughts. The smart phone can then store this information and remember the gear change for next time you are cycling over the same terrain.

Creating this new technology is allowing people to consider riding a bike as a more feasible method of transportation and is becoming more and more popular, being a type of transport that more people are choosing to use. With the creation of new innovations and fresh ideas being incorporated into the cycling world, riding a bike is no longer a travelling object of the past and is now seen as the thing to use when getting from A to B.

Wearing some form of protection on your head is a vital part of riding a bike and is a safety aspect that everyone should include into their riding habits. Obviously this exciting new product will not be available to everyone just yet so you may just have to cope with a basic style for now. Even so when purchasing a bike you need to add this level of protection to your list of accessories, as accidents can happen and a sore head isn't something anybody wants.

CONCLUSION

HOW TO READ A PERSON'S MIND DURING INTERVIEWS AND INTERROGATIONS

Who remembers the Gilligan's Island episode when Gilligan found a bush that had seeds, and when the castaway's ate them, they could read each other's mind? (Gilligan's Island, season 2, episode 19 which aired 01/27/66...Wikipedia has everything!) If that bush existed, would you be willing to eat the seeds and read everybody's mind?

If you do recall that episode, reading the minds of other people did not work out very well and caused a lot of interpersonal/relationship problems, and in the end, Gilligan set the bush on fire. As problematic as it may be for relationships, how GREAT would it be during investigative interviews and criminal interrogations! We can ask the ⬜uestions and know what they are thinking before they even answer, and then we can compare what is "in their mind" with what came "out of their mouth". We can have that ability to a certain degree. The ability to "read someone's mind" is not about mystical powers, tarot cards, crystal balls, or "memory seed bushes". It is about understanding people and behavior.

Specifically, it is about understanding each individual you are talking with and establishing rapport as well as establishing a baseline of behavior. Establishing rapport is essential to effective communication, whether it is an investigative interview or a criminal interrogation. Without rapport there will be a lack of trust, and without trust, how much information would you expect a person to provide? Especially is if is incriminating information, sensitive information or personal circumstances that they would rather not talk about but are highly relevant and valuable to the investigation. By establishing rapport we align ourselves with the individual, which increases trust and helps the communication and information flow.

As mentioned above, we also want to establish a baseline of behavior with each individual we talk with. A baseline is the "normal" behavioral, physical, linguistic and paralinguistic behavior of the individual when you are talking with them. How do they behave while answering questions? What do they do with their hands when responding? How do they position their feet throughout the interview? How do they align their torso with you? How about signs of nervousness; sweating, hives, carotid pulse on their neck? How about their eyes, tone of voice, specific words they use, emotions, etc. The list is virtually endless of all the available stimuli during an interview, which is why after a lengthy interview or interrogation, the interviewer is often physically and emotionally drained. However, not only do we have to be observant of the above signs as well as a slew of others, we have to be aware of changes in any of those as well. That is the crucial function of establishing a baseline, to see any deviations from it.

The baseline itself is not that important. If the person constantly tapped their foot throughout the interview that probably does not mean anything. However, if the person does not tap their foot at all (baseline) but then you ask questions about a particular topic and then she starts doing a tap-dance, you will be wise to revisit that topic again and probe deeply. Also, if she taps her foot constantly (baseline) but during a particular line of questioning, she locks her feet under the legs of her chair to try to stop them, that may be relevant as well. Again, it is changes in that particular person's baseline that is of interest to us and should help us focus our questioning.

By establishing rapport and a baseline we can see deviations in the baseline during the interview and then focus our ⬚uestioning around that area. Not only does this give us insight (mind reading) that there is an issue here, it makes the person also believe that we know more than we do because we keep coming back and driving questioning around that specific spot they want to avoid, or are reluctant to discuss. The same is true with linguistic characteristics within written statements. We may see the person writing about the event and using the pronoun "I" throughout their statement, then when they get to the main issue of the incident, the pronoun "I" disappears from the statement. What does that mean? It means that they are not committed to what they are saying at that particular area within the statement. We saw a change in their language use, and we focus on that spot in the statement with probing, information gather ⬚uestioning. Mind reading. They want to remove themselves from the story at that point, but we keep bringing them back with "tell me more about that..."

Well, it is not really mind reading, and of course we don't make any judgments about their innocence or guilt at this point, but when we establish rapport and a baseline with the people we ☐uestion, and look for deviations from that baseline as a focus-point for our ☐uestioning, we will be much more effective at gathering information and ultimately getting the truth, which is our ultimate goal.

www.ingramcontent.com/pod-product-compliance
Lightning Source LLC
Chambersburg PA
CBHW072041280526
45788CB00006B/2138